ADVERTISING
LAYOUT
TECHNIQUES

ADVERTISING LAYOUT TECHNIQUES

by HARRY BORGMAN

WATSON-GUPTILL PUBLICATIONS, NEW YORK

To Margaret Stein

Copyright © 1983 by Watson-Guptill Publications

First published 1983 in New York by Watson-Guptill Publications,
a division of Billboard Publications, Inc.,
1515 Broadway, New York, N.Y. 10036

Library of Congress Cataloging in Publication Data
Borgman, Harry.
Advertising layout techniques.
Includes index.
1. Advertising layout and typography. I. Title.
HF5825.B68 1983   659.13′24   83-1351
ISBN 0-8230-0154-7
Distributed in the United Kingdom by Phaidon Press Ltd., Littlegate
House, St. Ebbe's St., Oxford

Manufactured in U.S.A.

1 2 3 4 5 6 7 8 9/87 86 85 84 83

CONTENTS

ABOUT LAYOUT RENDERING

Many artists earn their living doing illustrations or renderings for advertising agencies. Much of this work is used in advertising layouts and other types of presentations made for the purpose of evaluating and discussing proposed advertising campaigns or ideas. Most layout work is involved with advertising media such as newspaper and magazine advertisements, television commercials, catalogs, brochures, and folders. This book is about this particular phase of the advertising business—doing presentation layout renderings—and the actual techniques and methods employed by artists who do this kind of work.

First, let me explain further just what a "layout" is. A layout is a kind of mock-up, or model, in the form of a sketch, drawing, or even a painting, of what a proposed advertisement might look like when it finally appears in a magazine, newspaper, or on television. This layout is produced by an advertising agency so that an idea for an ad campaign, catalog, or TV commercial can be visualized better by the client. The layouts are presented to the client and then evaluated prior to going to the expense of actually producing the final work. After this evaluation, any major or minor changes can be incorporated into the finished piece. The layout also might convince the client that the idea is simply no good and should not be followed through to final production. All advertising agencies must do these presentation layouts for their clients when submitting new ideas for advertising campaigns or any other work that is to be produced. Layouts can save a great deal of money, as well as time and effort. It is much cheaper to produce a layout than to go ahead and actually produce an ad or a TV commercial. This is the primary reason that this phase of the business exists, as the costs involved make it prohibitive to produce finished work for any kind of speculation. The fees charged by professional artists, photographers, and top models, as well as other related costs, cannot be incurred at the idea or development stage of advertising, and it simply makes good sense to submit layouts for approval.

There are different degrees of finish for layouts used for presentation. First, there is the idea rough, a quick sketch that the artist makes of the basic compositional arrangement. Next the artist does a semi-comprehensive layout, which is usually done spontaneously and, because it is done quickly, is fresher looking than the final layout will be. The next type of layout is the comprehensive. It is done tighter, with more detail and accuracy than the semi-comp. Both of these types of layouts are done with markers on layout paper. If an even tighter layout is required, then a painted comprehensive layout is done; often, for this kind of comp, the type and the headlines are set by a typographer or lettering service and then mounted right into position on the layout.

It is necessary to use layouts not only for printed ads but in any field where ideas must be presented or simulated visually. Television commercials also begin in the form of layouts called storyboards. A storyboard is a series of related pictures depicting what the action might be in the actual film when it is finally produced. In Hollywood, extensive storyboards are created to aid in the production of full-length feature films. Sales promotion companies also use layouts for many items they produce, such as direct-mail pieces, brochures, catalogs, counter displays, outdoor signs, and packaging. Companies that specialize in the development of corporate identity programs also rely on layouts to help sell their ideas.

Layout artists are employed not only by advertising agencies and sales promotion companies but also by art studios and some publishers as well. Some layout artists prefer to work on a freelance basis, as independent suppliers to the companies that are in need of this kind of work. One of the highest-paying areas for the layout artist is in the automotive industry. The manufacturers buy an enormous amount of material in layout form, either directly or through their advertising agencies, keeping a great many artists busy.

ABOUT THIS BOOK

The purpose of this book is to introduce you to the rendering of layouts for the advertising business. Many different types of layouts will be covered in detail, and examples of a great variety of work done in advertising will be illustrated. Art students and beginning layout renderers, as well as others involved in the advertising business, will find valuable information as well as a few ideas which may help to improve their own work.

The various tools, materials, media, and layout-rendering techniques are discussed in Part 1. Part 2 introduces and explains the nine basic stages a layout can go through before it is completed—from the initial research to a finished, painted comprehensive layout. Part 3 is devoted to ten detailed step-by-step demonstrations which graphically show the development of ideas, from the artist's first thoughts right through to finished layouts. In many instances, the finished printed piece is shown so that you can compare it with the first idea roughs. The last section, Part 4, consists of twelve typical layout assignments that demonstrate, step by step, the diversity of problem-solving techniques that can be used in a variety of assignments. The book concludes with some tips on how to get started in the field of advertising layout.

HOW TO USE THIS BOOK

To get the most out of this book, read it thoroughly and study all of the examples carefully. Practice the exercises, especially those dealing with markers, often. This will familiarize you with the primary tools used, better enabling you to understand how the examples shown in this book were done. The inexperienced student should realize that it will take a certain amount of time as well as practice to be able to use the tools properly. The best approach, of course, is to proceed slowly, being certain that you understand each exercise thoroughly before going on to the next one. Also keep in mind that there is a great deal of material presented here, and it will take a certain amount of time to absorb all of it. With a little patience and a lot of practice, you will be able to comprehend fully everything discussed in the book. Occasionally you should reexamine the step-by-step demonstrations; you will find them much clearer as you grow and develop.

If you first work in black and grays, leaving color for later, you will quickly gain the confidence needed to proceed to the much more complex work. Working with black and the grays will also afford you plenty of experience in handling the tools at this stage of your development. You can practice rendering copies of black-and-white photographs taken from newspapers or magazines, limiting your markers to black and grays no. 2 and no. 5. Do flat, simple renditions of the pictures without getting involved with subtle gradations of blended tones at the beginning. This same idea applies when you start working in color: keep things as simple as possible. As you progress, you can try more detailed, precise work, referring back to this book to reexamine some of the examples shown. Be sure not to throw away any of your earlier work. It is enlightening to compare the earlier renderings with your latest efforts and see the improvement you've made.

When practicing, don't limit your subject matter; strive for variety in this area. Render people, still lifes, portraits, animals, mechanical subjects, and scenes. The experience you gain through working on a variety of subjects will benefit you later when you begin working in the business. Markers work well for outdoor sketching, which is another way you can practice working with layout tools.

YOU AND THE ADVERTISING BUSINESS

Certain types of personalities lend themselves well to doing advertising layouts, and I would like to elaborate on this point a bit. Markers have a distinct quality about them that determines the way they must be used. They are basically a spontaneous medium, and a person who enjoys doing watercolor painting would also have a natural feeling for using markers. For best results, markers require bold handling and fast thinking, qualities which are also necessary for the person who works with watercolors.

As far as advertising is concerned, personality also can enter the picture. The advertising business is not for everyone, as it requires the artist to work quickly and under fairly adverse conditions. A good deal of the work in this business is done under less-than-ideal conditions—and often, under great pressure. People who are not temperamental are those best suited for the advertising business, as the artist is often required to work when he or she least feels like it, including weekends and even overnight. An advertising artist must be willing to sacrifice some personal time and to work odd hours. Another obvious qualification for the business is being able to draw fairly well—and a good sense of color is also advantageous.

Another very important requirement for the advertising business is that the quality of your work must remain consistent, even under the demands and pressures of tight deadlines. In other words, if you are doing a whole series of ads or storyboard frames, all of the renderings should be of the same high quality. Some renderings cannot be looser than others, as consistency is not only important but expected.

You should be self-motivated and enjoy the advertising business. As a layout artist you will often be asked to create a presentation that conveys a mood, an idea, or a concept; this requires ability, interest, creativity, and a thorough knowledge of the business itself. These requirements, as well as the deadline problems, may seem overwhelming, but you can develop yourself as an artist and become proficient in the technical aspects over a period of time, through experience and practice. And there are compensations, too—for a good professional layout artist can be in great demand and earn a very good living.

PART 1

TOOLS AND EXERCISES

There are specific materials universally used for producing advertising layouts, most of the work being done using markers on layout paper. To a lesser degree, illustration board is used with painting media such as gouache, watercolors, inks, dyes, and acrylic paint. The standard marker is a remarkable drawing and rendering tool, but a certain amount of practice is necessary to develop confidence and proficiency in this medium. The practice exercises suggested in this section will be a valuable aid for developing your skills with markers as well as the other media.

MARKERS AND MARKER PENS

The most basic and important layout tool is the marker. Marker is the ideal medium for working quickly, and this probably accounts for its great popularity in the advertising business. Markers dry quickly, are compatible with other media, and are available in a seemingly limitless color range. In addition, they are convenient to use, requiring no mixing trays, water bowls, brushes, or messy cleanup. Markers come with different nib shapes, the standard one being the wedge type. Others are bullet-shaped, and some are fine-pointed types. I use the wedge-shaped nibs for just about all of my work, but occasionally I use the other types as well.

There are many fine brands of markers available, and they come in all shapes and sizes. I would suggest that you buy one or two markers of each of the brands that feel right in your hand, and then work with these at home. You will soon be able to decide which type you prefer, and then you can purchase more colors individually or perhaps even in a set. Once you decide which brand you like the best, it would be wise to stick to that brand so that you can get used to the way it works and to its color range. Some of the major brands of markers available at most artist supply stores are Ad Markers, Design Art Markers, Magic Markers, and Pantone, all of which have extensive color ranges. I have used most types of markers, and I personally prefer the Berol Magic Marker brand, which offers a tremendous range of colors—186 in all.

One unique advantage which the Magic Marker has over the other brands is that the bottle cap can be opened easily, enabling you to remove the inner core, a fibrous material containing the color. This inner core can be used on its side to paint very large areas of color smoothly, something which is rather difficult to accomplish with the normal nib. You should remove the inner core with a pair of needle-nosed pliers; you can then hold the core with the pliers to cover large areas with tone.

If you buy Magic Markers, you might start out with a set of basic colors and a Complementary/Plus set of colors. The basic set consists of vermilion, chrome orange, lemon yellow, yellow green, forest green, Prussian blue, light blue, ultramarine, violet, burnt sienna, pink, and black. The Complementary/Plus set includes pale sepia, sepia, sand, crimson, pale blue, process blue, lavender, pale olive, olive, aqua, pale yellow, and sanguine. A valuable addition to these two sets would be a set of cool grays, or you can buy just a few—nos. 2, 3, 5, and 7.

In addition to the regular markers, marker pens are also used extensively for layout rendering. The Pilot, Stabilo, and Pentel brands are all excellent drawing tools. I use the ones with the extra-fine tips for many of my basic outline drawings.

Markers are available with many different kinds of nibs, the standard one having the multi-faceted wedge shape made from a felt material. Other useful nibs are the fine-pointed types, which are usually made from nylon or plastic.

PANTONE 415-F   PANTONE 466-M   LINER   MARK

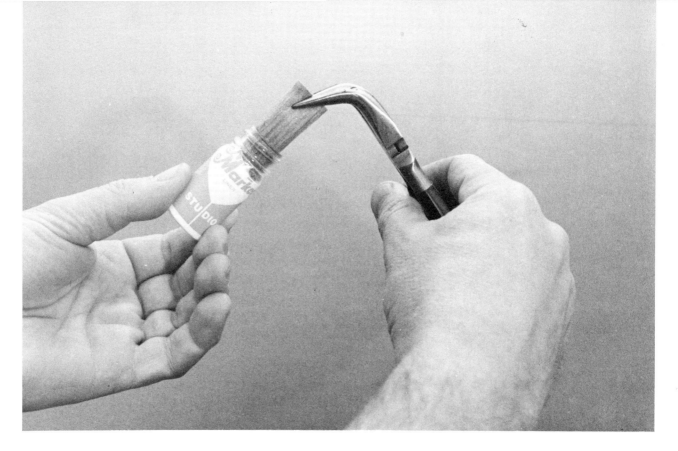

The Magic Marker Studio brand has the advantage of a removable cap, which enables you to remove the inner core containing the color. This core can be held with needle-nosed pliers for rendering large areas.

PENCILS

For general purposes, such as sketching or doing underlay drawings, you will need a good-quality graphite pencil such as the Berol Eagle Turquoise, Koh-I-Noor, Mars-Lumograph, or Venus brands. I generally use pencil leads of three different degrees of hardness: the 2H, HB, and the softer 2B, but you may prefer some of the other grades. There are other pencils that also will prove very useful—such as the Berol Prismacolor pencils, which have a wax-type lead. I have used this line for many years and find it to be of the highest quality and consistency. These pencils are available in a wide assortment of sixty colors, and their leads are smooth and strong enough to sharpen to a very fine point. Prismacolor pencils can be purchased singly or in sets of twelve, twenty-four, thirty-six, forty-eight, or sixty colors. Also included in their color range are cool and warm grays, which I find very useful. These pencils are very compatible with markers on layout paper or with paint on illustration board. Another interesting pencil is the water-soluble type; it is similar to the wax-type pencil in that it can be used with markers, dyes, inks, and paint. The big difference between them is that the lines drawn with a water-soluble pencil can be dissolved by washing clear water over them, thereby creating interesting effects. A few of the water-soluble types of pencils are the Mongol "Paint with Pencils" brand, the All-Stabilo, and the Caran D'Ache Prismalo brand. These are all available individually or in boxed sets of different colors.

GOUACHE

Gouache, also known as designers' colors, is used extensively for illustration and also for painting comp layouts. This medium is quite versatile, as the colors can be used very wet, like watercolors, or in an opaque manner. You can even paint opaque washes with gouache. The most popular brand is Winsor & Newton Designers' Gouache because of its high quality. I have used these colors for many years, and I highly recommend this brand. They are available in a wide range of eighty colors, but you can get along easily with just a few colors. It is wise not to keep too many tubes of colors on hand, as they might dry out and become unusable. Your best bet is to buy an introductory set, which will serve you nicely. The introductory set contains ten assorted colors, including permanent white, lemon yellow, spectrum yellow, spectrum red, ultramarine, spectrum violet, alizarin crimson, sky blue, brilliant green, and ivory black. You might start out with gouache by just using the black and white, painting with tones of grays mixed from these, until you become more familiar with them.

ACRYLIC COLORS

Acrylic polymer emulsion paints are widely used by many advertising artists as well as fine artists. Acrylics are quite different from other water-base paints, as they dry waterproof and will not dissolve when painted over as other water media do. Acrylics are a highly versatile medium and can be used in a surprising variety of ways—in transparent washes, like watercolors; opaque, like gouache; or very thickly, like oils, for impasto effects. Two of the best brands of acrylics available are Liquitex, manufactured by Permanent Pigments, and Hyplar, made by Grumbacher; both are available in tubes and jars of varying sizes. For your purposes the smaller tubes would be preferable. Again, as I suggested doing with gouache, start out by using mars black and titanium white, painting with mixtures of these until you get used to working with the acrylics. Then you can purchase a basic set of colors and practice with these.

OTHER USEFUL PAINTING MEDIA

Painted comp layouts can also be done with watercolors, inks, dyes, or a combination of all of these media. Watercolors are available in tubes or in boxed sets of hard cakes of color, whereas dyes and inks are available in bottles.

BRUSHES

Buy only the highest-quality brushes, as the cheaper variety will just not work satisfactorily and will not last very long; in the long run, they will cost you more. I would recommend a high-quality brush such as the Winsor & Newton Albata (Series 7) sable, or a comparable brand. You will need several different sizes but can start with nos. 3, 5, and 7.

WORKING SURFACES

The surface most commonly used for marker rendering is layout paper. There are many kinds of layout paper available, but be sure to use only the highest-quality paper, as you will probably be disappointed in your work on the cheaper papers. Check with your local art supply stores; they will be able to advise you on which layout papers are the best. Bienfang makes a high-quality paper which is available in different size pads: 9″ x 12″ (23 x 30 cm), 11″ x 14″ (28 x 36 cm), 14″ x 17″ (36 x 43 cm), and 19″ x 24″ (48 x 61 cm). For doing underlay drawings and idea doodles, you can use tracing paper, which is less expensive but sufficient for these purposes. For doing painted comprehensive layouts, you should use a good-quality illustration board. These boards are available in a variety of sizes and usually in three different surfaces: rough, hot-pressed (very smooth), and cold-pressed (slightly grained). Cold-pressed surfaces are those most commonly used for doing painted comp layouts and other illustrations.

OTHER USEFUL EQUIPMENT

Color-film sheets are special pressure-sensitive, adhesive-backed sheets for use in the preparation of layouts. These sheets are available in a wide range of colors and can be cut to the required shape or size with an X-acto knife. Another very useful item is dry-transfer lettering, which is available in a variety of typefaces and innumerable sizes. Most transfer letters come in black, but some faces are available in white and red as well. These letters are transferred easily to layouts to create a very finished, professional look. If you have to draw circles or ovals, there is nothing as easy as using circle and oval templates. French curves are handy guides for drawing or inking curved lines or shapes. For ruling, squaring up ads, and drawing parallel lines for things such as in ruled copy blocks, a T-square and a triangle are invaluable. When drawing with graphite, pastels, or pastel pencils, you will need to spray your work with fixative so it will not smudge. Fixative is available in either a mat or gloss finish, the mat being preferable for your purposes. X-acto knives are very useful for trimming layout renderings or cutting layouts to size. The blades come in several different shapes, but the no. 11 is the best for your use. For attaching layout paper to your drawing board or reference material to the board or wall, masking tape works the best. To point your pencil lead after sharpening away the surrounding wood with the X-acto knife, use a sanding block. For erasing small areas, a kneaded eraser is best, as it can be easily shaped. Other types of erasers, such as the Pink Pearl and the plastic types, are quite useful. For mixing colors, a palette with individual wells is very good, but you might also want a larger butcher-type enameled tray. There are occasions when you will be required to photograph your own reference material. It would be a good idea for you to own either a Polaroid camera or a 35mm single lens reflex camera. My Polaroid 180 camera, by giving me results immediately, enables me to get right to work on an assignment.

PROJECTORS

I use a Beseler Vu-Lyte II opaque-type projector to blow up photographs or other material, and this can be a great time-saver. Drawings done from these projected images need not be perfect, as long as the proportions are correct. Then, when the drawing is redone for the layout, it can be drawn more accurately. Often clients provide the artist

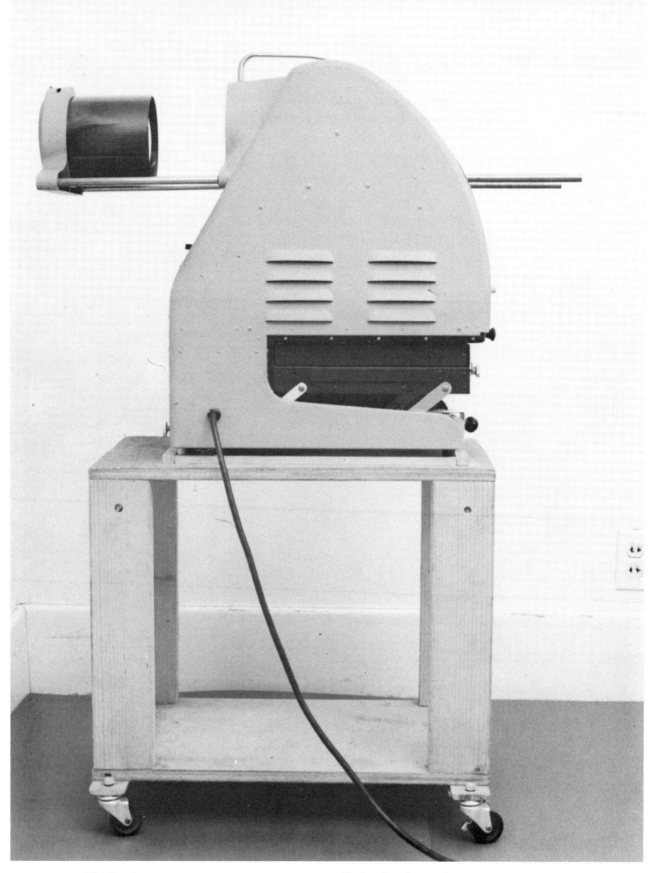

The Beseler Vu-Lyte II opaque projector is mounted on a wooden stand with wheels for easy movement. The projector shown here is equipped with an attachment that allows the lens barrel to slide out of its mount on spe-cially fitted guides, enabling the user to proj-ect images reduced in size from the original. This reducing attachment is not standard equipment, but it was added by the Lewis Artist Supply Company of Detroit, Michigan.

with reference material in the form of a 35mm color slide. These slides can be blown up to size using a normal 35mm slide projector, and an accurate diagram of the object can be traced in just a few seconds, saving valuable time. The drawing table I use is perfect for projecting, as it is counter-balanced so that it can be tilted easily to an upright position, in which it locks automatically. I can project the material onto a sheet of paper that has been taped to the board surface. If you do not own an elaborate drawing table such as this, you can do the same thing by projecting the images onto a wall or some other vertical surface.

EXERCISES

The following exercises are designed to acquaint you with all of the different drawing and painting tools which are used for layout rendering. These exercises may appear at first to be quite simple, but you should still do all of them, as they will help you to learn about the tools you will be using. Pens, pencils, markers, and the painting media all handle quite differently, and the exercises will help you to understand the possibilities as well as the limitations of each medium. After practicing the exercises thoroughly, go beyond the exercises and experiment on your own. Be sure to practice a great deal, as this is the only way you can learn to master your tools and materials.

WATER-SOLUBLE MARKERS

Tools: Pilot Fineliner or Razor Point pen; Pentel Sign Pen; sheet of layout paper; sheet of rough watercolor paper; red sable watercolor brush, no. 5 or 7.

As shown in the top left example, practice drawing various straight lines on the layout paper with the Pilot pen. Next draw a series of loops and circles, drawing quickly, freely, and without hesitation. Then concentrate on drawing different textures; try creating tones made up of short, dashlike strokes or even dot patterns. You can create tone by drawing lines over one another at right angles; this is called crosshatching. Try to space the lines evenly so that you achieve a uniform crosshatch tone.

Now try the same exercises again, this time with the Pentel Sign Pen, which will create a darker, heavier line. This is shown in the top right example.

On the lower half of the group shown, I have drawn the same lines and tonal effects on watercolor paper, again using both types of pens. Then I have washed clear water over these strokes and lines, dissolving them into tones. This technique can be useful for doing certain kinds of painted comprehensive layouts.

The finer-pointed pens are excellent for doing basic outline drawings, and the Pentel Sign Pen is quite good for filling in large areas.

The tone here was much too dark, and I lightened it a bit, using a medium gray Prismacolor pencil. The details were then drawn back in with the Pentel pen.

These short Pentel pen strokes create a grassy texture.

Here I used a Fineline pen to draw zigzag strokes that simulate grass.

You can see how the Pentel Sign Pen strokes were dissolved into tones by washing clear water over them. I used a no. 7 red sable brush here.

NON-SOLUBLE MARKERS

> Tools: Design Art Marker 229 LU; Markette Thinrite marker; black Magic Marker with standard nib; sheet of layout paper.

Draw various types of lines and textures as shown on the top left, using the Design Art Marker. This pen is a very handy tool with a hard, fine point.

Next, with the Markette pen, draw lines and textures as shown on the top right. Solid areas of tone can be done with this pen also. Note that the lines drawn with the Markette pen are much heavier than those drawn with the Design Art Marker.

In the lower section are some of the lines and textures that can be drawn using a standard Magic Marker. The multi-faceted wedge-shaped nib is a remarkable drawing tool, capable of making a great variety of lines of varying weights, as well as many textural effects. The first series of lines was drawn with the fine edge of the marker nib. If you look closely at the nib, you will see two other surfaces with which you can draw heavier lines. By just holding the marker in different positions you can create countless textures and a great variety of linear effects. Experiment to see how many different textures you can achieve with this tool.

See how a fine-line pen was used to draw the lightest area of the animal's hair.

A Pentel Sign Pen, which draws a bolder line, was used for the darker, medium-weight lines.

A black Magic Marker was used to draw these heavier, darker strokes on the animal as well as to indicate the leaves.

Notice how the fine-line pen was used over the leaves, creating a gray tone through cross-hatching.

The background tone was created by ruling in medium-weight, uniform lines. This evenness helps to keep the tone the same value. A Pentel Sign Pen was used, with a triangle serving as a straightedge.

TOOLS AND EXERCISES

MAGIC MARKERS, FLAT AND BLENDED TONES

Tools: Magic Markers, black and cool grays no. 1, 3, 5, and 7; sheet of layout paper.

To practice rendering flat tones, try doing small areas at first, and then attempt larger panels of tone. You will be able to render flat tones more successfully if you work rather fast, as working slowly can cause an overlap of tone with an uneven effect. The lighter tones are easier to render smoothly than the darker ones, but with a little practice you should be able to accomplish this.

On the lower half of the illustration you see a series of blended tones. Start with the no. 1 gray, and while this tone is still wet, add the no. 3, and then the 5, 7, and black. Keep practicing until you are able to render a perfectly blended tone. You will see that working quickly is the best method, as the tones must be blended while they are still wet. After you are able to blend the markers successfully into a smooth, continuous tone, try doing it on a much larger area.

Here is a flat tone that was put in the background with a no. 3 gray Magic Marker.

These dark gray and black marker tones were blended to help create the illusion of form.

A Pentel pen was used in this area over a flat gray tone to indicate the proper texture.

This leatherlike texture was added over a flat gray tone with a Pentel Sign Pen.

Notice how I indicated a few details with a light gray Prismacolor pencil.

WAX PENCILS

Tools:	Prismacolor pencils: black 935, white 938, cold gray medium 966, and cold gray light 968; black and gray Magic Markers; layout paper.

Wax-type pencils can be used to lighten, darken, or even smooth out marker tones. They are also excellent for blending and for adding detail, such as textures or highlights, to renderings.

Try drawing various pencil strokes as shown in the top section of these examples. Practice drawing light tones over dark tones, and vice versa. Try drawing various textural effects, as well as crosshatching. Try blending a pencil tone from very light to dark, and then do the same thing using various grays and black.

In the lower area, Prismacolor pencils have been used in conjunction with markers. On the left, marker tones have been blended with the pencil tones, a very useful technique for layout rendering. Practice drawing with these pencils over various marker tones, trying different textural and linear effects. After you become familiar with this technique, you can try some experiments with colored pencils over colored marker tones.

Gray Prismacolor pencil lines drawn loosely over flat marker tones give the illusion of speed.

See how effectively a marker tone can be blended by using a medium gray Prismacolor pencil.

This shading in the darker gray areas was also done using a gray Prismacolor pencil.

WATERCOLORS AND DYES

> Tools: A tube of ivory black watercolor; Higgins water-soluble ink; cold-pressed illustration board; a no. 5 or 7 red sable watercolor brush.

Comprehensive layouts can be done with watercolors, inks (or dyes), or a combination of the two on illustration board. The basic exercises shown here are almost the same as those for the markers. First, try painting a flat tone with a wash of diluted ivory black. This is accomplished most easily by dampening the illustration board surface first with a wash of clear water. Next, try blending a tone from black to pure white. Try these exercises on a small scale at first, and then try them on larger areas. The middle section shows a flatly painted wash of gray with washes of black painted over. Try variations of this by letting the basic wash dry a little more and by using wetter and dryer washes of tone over this.

In the lower left area, different lines and textures, including a dry-brush effect, have been done with the paint.

The lower center section shows the effect of painting strokes over a wash tone while it is still wet. Try this by working over various tones in different stages of drying. The lower right area is made up of different strokes of wash tones over one another. Be careful to observe how the paint reacts in all of these examples, as these are effects which you may want to duplicate when working on a rendering. Do all of the same exercises with dyes and water-soluble inks.

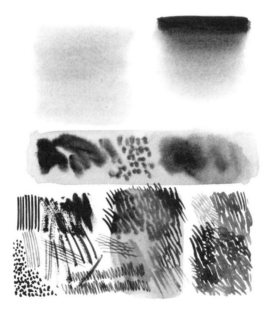

See how the leaves have been indicated with a brush, using only short strokes and a gray wash over the sky tone.

This sky tone is a flat wash of diluted ivory black that has been applied with a no. 9 red sable brush.

This tone on the building was blended by washing a darker tone over a lighter tone while it was still wet. The stone texture was added after the washes were completely dry.

Drybrush lines were used here to indicate the branches of a bush.

Small strokes were painted in to stimulate the texture of grass. These strokes were made with a darker wash over a lighter background tone.

GOUACHE

Tools: Winsor & Newton Designers' Gouache, ivory black and permanent white; cold-pressed illustration board; a no. 5 or 7 red sable watercolor brush.

These exercises are similar to the previous ones, but will also include opaque paint and pencils used with gouache. In the upper left is a flat wash of the ivory black, and on the right is a blended tone. The next section has a wash tone consisting of a mixture of ivory black and permanent white. This tone was painted over a previously dampened area of the illustration board. Note that Prismacolor gray and white pencils were used over this wash when it dried. The area on the right was done by painting blobs of opaque tone over a wet wash of clear water.

In the third section of this exercise, on the left, a flat opaque tone has been painted. Prismacolor pencils were used to draw various tones, lines, and textures over this tone. The section to the right of this area shows a blended opaque tone done with mixtures of ivory black and permanent white.

The lower section shows a flat opaque tone into which black was brushed while it was still damp, creating a slight wash effect. In the middle, the same thing was done with the white paint. The end area shows black painted lines, textures, and drybrush painted over the opaque tone. Do all of these exercises until you become familiar with this medium.

An opaque wash tone was mixed from permanent white and ivory black and then painted on the background. The upper section of the background was painted with a darker mixture and pure black.

Notice how a light gray Prismacolor pencil has been used to define the side and rim as well as to indicate reflections. The pencil also has been used to lighten an area near the center of the glass.

These opaque wash tones have been roughly blended while still wet.

Some tones were created by using drybrush strokes.

ACRYLIC PAINT

Tools: Liquitex titanium white and mars black acrylic paints; illustration board, hot- or cold-pressed; a no. 5 or 7 red sable watercolor brush.

Acrylics are similar to gouache, but they do have other qualities, such as the fact that they dry waterproof. This means that when you paint over previously painted areas, the tones will not dissolve as they do with other paint media. Do all of the same exercises with the acrylics as you have for all the other media. Begin by painting a flat area, using a wash of the black; then try a blended wash. Work over washes with darker and lighter washes, and then mix tones of the black and white. Practice with opaque washes as you did with the designers' colors. Try painting opaque washes over non-opaque washes, and then paint opaque washes over other opaque washes. At the bottom of the page I painted an opaque area and then painted other opaque tones over it while the background was still wet, causing the tones to blend slightly. Then I painted a darker gray tone with a thicker mixture of paint, creating a drybrush effect. Next I painted a dark gray tone over the background, and then lighter grays. Try painting a flat gray tone, and when it is dry, work over this with Prismacolor pencils using the black, white, and grays. After you feel familiar with this medium, you can do all the same exercises using colored paints and pencils.

Here a wash of mars black has been painted on the hair.

Over the black wash, light gray Prismacolor pencil lines have been used for the hair texture.

In this area, an opaque wash of a mixture of titanium white and mars black has been painted.

Notice how a light gray wash tone has been painted on the face, and over this, opaque tones and white highlights have been added.

To darken the shadow area on the face, a medium gray Prismacolor pencil was used.

PART 2

DEVELOPMENT OF A LAYOUT ASSIGNMENT

The purpose of this section is to clarify the various stages through which an artist might be required to take an advertising layout assignment. I have chosen to illustrate the stages with examples from a single project—a page of an automotive catalog designed for AMC/Renault—which will enable you to follow the nine basic stages a layout can go through, from idea doodle to painted comprehensive layout. This part of the assignment was quite complicated, as it depicts some of the high points in the history of the diversified French manufacturer.

Most assignments are much simpler and do not require as many stages of development before completion, but because of its complications, this project will be more interesting to you as a potential layout artist. It was certainly interesting to me, and I enjoyed doing all the necessary research for the finished layout. By searching through books and magazines, I was able to gather enough information and photographic material for the assignment. Fortunately, I located a local bookstore that specializes in material on automotive and aviation history, and this simplified my job a great deal.

You will notice, when looking over these examples, that I have used different materials for doing my basic idea roughs—sometimes pencils, and in other instances, marker pens. These drawing tools can be used on either layout paper or tracing paper, for at this stage it really doesn't matter. Tracing paper, however, is much cheaper than layout paper and can be used for many of the early phases of layout development, including the underlay drawing.

As I progress to the preliminary rough stage, I prefer to work with marker pens and Magic Markers on layout paper, as these sketches are often shown to the client. Layouts done this way are more detailed and finished, and therefore they are much easier for the client to visualize than the earlier idea-rough stages.

The next stage is the semi-comprehensive layout, which is done even more carefully than the preliminary rough. After that, the comprehensive layout follows; this is much more refined, though often the only difference between the two is whether the type on the ad has been hand-lettered or typeset and mounted into position. The last stage of development is usually the painted comprehensive layout, which is done with paint on illustration board rather than with markers on layout paper. The reason for painting layouts is because an artist can produce a much more finished job with paint than can be accomplished with markers. In other instances, very tight comprehensive layouts might be done by mounting a print of the actual photograph to be used into the layout. This kind of layout is very difficult to distinguish from the printed ad.

NECESSARY REFERENCE MATERIAL. Most assignments require the artist to use some visual reference material. This is quite important, as you really can't count on your memory or attempt to guess at what something looks like. Reference material is especially important when it comes to drawing a product, as the client knows it well, and it had better be accurate. Since products must be portrayed with accuracy, clients often will furnish you with either good photographic references or with the product itself, which you can photograph in the correct view. Reference material also can be found in libraries, book shops, specialized magazine stores, certain museums, and even in corporate publications or displays. This particular assignment required a great deal of research so I could include all of the diverse activities in which the Renault Company has been involved over the years.

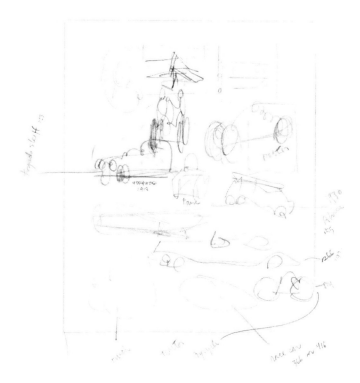

IDEA DOODLE. An idea doodle is a graphic representation of the artist's initial thoughts about an assignment. This is how most artists start to solve a design or illustration problem. In this particular case, having many elements to deal with, I found it essential to do a quick sketch of a basic compositional arrangement. A rough doodle like this is invaluable, as it not only helps the artist to grasp the problem mentally, but also is an aid in deciding which elements might be emphasized visually. With this idea doodle, I was starting to establish the composition, an important factor in the assignment. This kind of a rough is really a very crude, though sufficient, diagram—but usually it is not shown to a client, who may have difficulty deciphering it. Such doodles, of course, can be drawn on any kind of paper, with pencils or even marking pens.

IDEA-ROUGH SKETCH. The next stage is to do a slightly more accurate kind of a rough. This one was done on tracing paper with a Markette Thinrite marker, and it is what I call an idea-rough sketch because it is beyond the doodle stage. The basic composition is emerging, and the sketch has been developed enough to show most clients—especially since it will be presented with the reference material that has been gathered. Notice that on the margins of this sketch, I have noted the page numbers from the reference books so that they can be found again easily. My client agreed with the montage idea, and this sketch was used as a basis for further development.

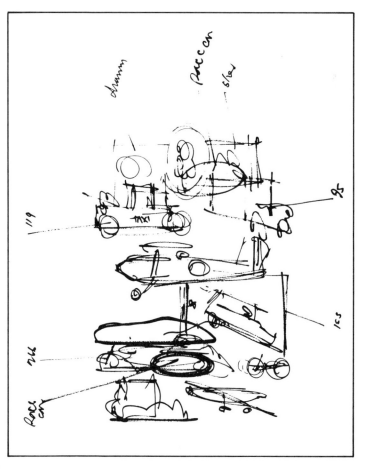

DEVELOPMENT OF A LAYOUT ASSIGNMENT

PRELIMINARY ROUGH SKETCH (above). In the previous example, the idea-rough sketch, I developed the basic composition for this illustration. Since the idea rough had been done only in line, I now needed to develop it further, this time utilizing gray tones as well as line. I call this stage a preliminary rough sketch, as it actually is the sketch that normally precedes the semi-comprehensive layout stage. Compare this preliminary rough with the previous one, and you will see that this rough is much easier to comprehend, as the various elements are beginning to take on more accurate shapes and their placement in the composition is more precise. By this stage I have also decided which of the items will be emphasized, which will be drawn in outline form, and where backgrounds might be appropriate. This preliminary rough sketch was done using marker pens and Magic Marker grays on layout paper. Following a discussion of this sketch with my client, it was decided to add more elements.

REVISED ROUGH SKETCH (right). Often at this early stage of the development of an assignment, the client wants to make changes or additions. This is precisely why it is important and wise to do preliminary work, as any changes or new elements can be added much more easily now than when the job is in a more advanced stage of completion. This kind of diagram is called a revised rough sketch. On this sketch, my client suggested that I add a Mack truck (a company that had recently been acquired by Renault) and perhaps another type of aircraft because of the company's involvement in that area during the early part of its history. I was also to include some kind of a farm vehicle and a car-carrier truck. The race car was to be eliminated and the dump truck, minimized in importance.

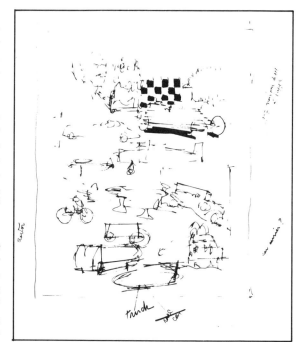

PRELIMINARY ROUGH SKETCH WITH COR-RECTIONS. Here I have used the revised preliminary rough sketch as a basis for a new preliminary rough, this time using marker pen and Magic Marker grays on tracing paper. By comparing this new sketch with the first preliminary rough on page 38, you can see that this one has been done with more accu-racy, and many of the products contain a greater amount of detail. I also minimized the World War I fighter aircraft and added a commercial mail plane, as this was an impor-tant Renault development. Remember that this rough was done because of the addition of new products, which required a change in the overall composition.

DEVELOPMENT OF A LAYOUT ASSIGNMENT

PENCIL UNDERLAY DRAWING. In order to produce the next stage of this assignment— the semi-comprehensive layout—properly, I found it necessary to do an accurate pencil underlay drawing of the composition, which would be used as a guide. The underlay drawing was done by projecting the reference material to size with a Beseler opaque projector and then tracing the images. Drawings like this can be done rather roughly, but the proportions of the objects must be very accurate. Projecting the reference material helps greatly in composing a complex illustration that consists of many elements. When this underlay drawing was complete, I slipped this drawing under a sheet of semi-transparent layout paper and then traced the image with a technical pen (a fine marker can also be used for this) before adding the various color tones.

MAGIC MARKER SEMI-COMPREHENSIVE LAYOUT. A semi-comprehensive layout is one that portrays all of the elements in a very recognizable state. In this particular case, I also used color, since the final printed piece would be produced in full color. The semi-comprehensive layout establishes the elements, their relative sizes, and the composition. Although the color may undergo some changes at a further stage of development, everything else should have been firmly established for now. This layout was shown to my client and was approved for development as a comprehensive layout.

MAGIC MARKER COMPREHENSIVE LAY-OUT. A comprehensive layout is done much more accurately and includes more details than the semi-comprehensive layout. It is started in much the same manner as the semi-comp, that is, by doing a tracing of the underlay pencil drawing—but this time, the drawing is traced more accurately. I even use a triangle for ruling in the straight lines, as well as circle and oval template guides for appropriate areas. After the line work is finished, I carefully fill in the objects, using col-ored Magic Markers. I try to be careful not to overwork any areas so that the colors remain clean and crisp. Markers can take on a drab and muddy appearance when they are worked over too much. It is best to work rapidly, keeping your color tones simple to achieve the freshest effects. As I rendered the products to be illustrated in this assignment, I carefully checked my reference material in order to maintain accuracy. I also make any necessary color changes.

PAINTED COMPREHENSIVE LAYOUT. This layout was done on cold-pressed illustration board, using the Magic Marker comprehensive layout as a guide for color. First, I did a pencil drawing of all of the elements in their correct positions by projecting the reference material directly onto the illustration board with the Beseler opaque projector. After making this rough drawing, I redrew all of the objects accurately, using a 2H graphite pencil and checking my reference material carefully. This pencil drawing was then inked with a technical pen, after which the color rendering was done by washing in tones of colored inks, dyes, and designers' colors. I added the color panels behind the transmission drawing and the desert vehicle with pieces of a transparent color film called Letratone. I used oval and circle guides as well as French curves to ink the drawing, and a triangle edge for the straight lines. This illustration is shown in color on page 128.

PART 3

STEP-BY-STEP DEMONSTRATIONS

This section consists of ten demonstrations that show clearly, step by step, just how a particular layout rendering or design was thought out and the various phases required for completion. In the more advanced of these demonstrations, I have included, whenever possible, all of the preliminary work that preceded the actual rendering. In a few cases, I have included the photographic reference material that was used. The first demonstration deals with the development of an automotive catalog, from first idea rough through preliminary rough sketches. Demonstration 2 is also involved with a catalog, but it shows a more advanced kind of rough and the stages from the preliminary rough layout through to the semi-comprehensive layout. Following this are examples of semi-comprehensive magazine ad layouts, which are covered in Demonstrations 3 and 4. Next a further layout development is presented, the comprehensive layout. This phase is explained in Demonstrations 5 through 8. Demonstration 9 is involved with the most finished type of layout, the painted comprehensive. TV storyboard renderings are discussed in the last demonstration. I have attempted to include a wide variety of subject matter in this group so you can get a better cross section of the material a layout artist deals with.

Study these demonstrations very carefully and review them occasionally. You can employ the information and methods presented in them when you do your own practice renderings—or even when you are doing an assignment. Everything shown in the demonstrations can be applied to your own work.

IDEA ROUGHS TO PRELIMINARY ROUGH
AUTOMOTIVE CATALOG

This demonstration will show the design development of an automotive catalog, from cover design to interior pages. Most of the renderings shown are in a form which I call idea roughs.

Idea roughs are something most artists do when they start a painting, illustration, or commercial assignment. It is very important to get something visual down on paper, no matter how roughly it is done, so that the idea can be evaluated. Many problems can be solved at this early stage which could otherwise crop up later when you are well into the project. The idea rough can be an important, time-saving step and you should get used to starting assignments and other projects by doing them. The last rough shown is more finished, and it is called a preliminary rough layout because it is the preliminary stage to doing more finished layouts in the form of semi-comprehensive or comprehensive layouts. Preliminary roughs are usually rendered in color as well, if the finished piece is going to appear in color.

STEP 1. There are many problems to deal with when you design a catalog because of the various elements which must be considered, the most important ones being the cover, continuity of the interior design and the flexibility of the design format itself. This last point is very important, as invariably some pictorial material, type, or charts will be added or dropped from the book during its development. Since a designer does not have a crystal ball, these inevitable changes must be anticipated. Shown here are my first idea roughs for the cover design. The client requested that two vehicles be shown, and at this stage I was trying to determine the exact car views to be used.

STEP 2 (left). In the first rough I showed the vehicles without a background, which was not very interesting. I tried another rough, this time including a very modern house in the background; this works better, as the picture composition is more interesting. This rough was also done in color so that the vehicle and background colors could be established.

STEP 3 (below). I liked the car views, but I was still not too pleased with the background situation, and I wanted to develop something a little more dramatic and exciting. In this new rough, I incorporated a large modern outdoor sculpture, which I felt added a great deal to the scene. I also lowered the lettering and used it in white rather than black. I also indicated how the rear cover would appear; it was to consist primarily of specifications on a gray toned background. You will notice that each time I do a progressive rough, the design and idea become clearer.

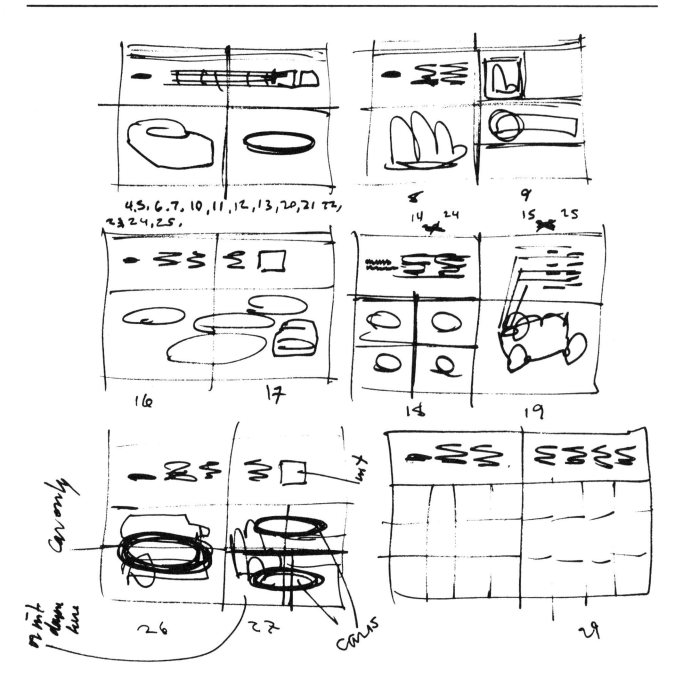

STEP 4. Having pretty much solved the cover design, I now needed to determine the direction of the interior pages. On a sheet of layout paper I began to sketch out the various pages, based on information provided by my client as to exactly what must appear on each page. This step was really a matter of organization, the assembling and sorting out of all the material. These kinds of sketches, or idea doodles, as I call them, aid a designer greatly because they help in organizing a complicated project and are something concrete that can be evaluated before proceeding to the next design phase.

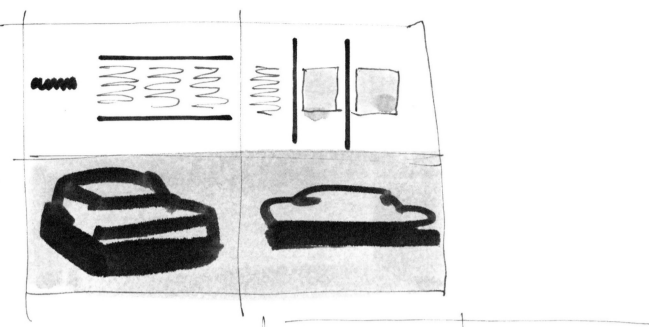

STEP 5. Next, to clarify my thinking and develop the page designs further, I did some slightly tighter versions, which I call idea-rough sketches. In these roughs, I used tones and even determined which vehicle views would be used. I also tried a design motif, in the form of type rules or bars, around the copy blocks and minor pictures. This motif, when used throughout the catalog, would help to create design continuity.

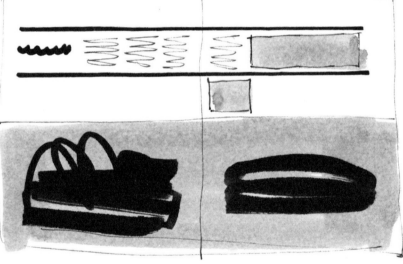

STEP 6 (above). Now that I was on the right track, I needed to do a larger, more accurate preliminary rough sketch to be sure the idea would hold up well in the larger scale. This was done half scale, 9¼'' x 5⅞'' (23.5 x 14.5 cm). I did a more detailed sketch showing a car with a sleek jet fighter aircraft in the background. This more detailed rough, also done in color, helped me to evaluate the design concept and determine whether it should be developed further.

STEP 7 (right). I was pleased with the previous rough, and so next I did a full-size 18½'' x 11¼'' (47 x 28.5 cm) preliminary rough of one of the other spreads so I could see how the pages would look when printed. In this new layout I could see exactly how large the vehicles would appear, and I could begin to consider the content of the backgrounds on the illustrations. The picture on the left-hand page shows a car on a blacktop road, a sunset in the background, and the suggestion of a distant hill or stretch of land across a lake or bay. The illustration on the right shows a direct side view of a car parked on a dry lake in Southern California. The smaller illustrations at the top show a tachometer and a performance shot of a car on a test track. I lettered the word *Spirit* with a Pentel pen and simulated the body-copy blocks by cutting type out of a magazine and mounting it in position on the layout. The overall effect gives a good impression of what the final page spread would look like.

PRELIMINARY ROUGH SKETCHES TO SEMI-COMPREHENSIVE LAYOUTS

CATALOG LAYOUT RENDERINGS

After the basic design concept of a catalog or brochure has been determined, the layout must be prepared for presentation to the client. Because the earliest layout developments, the idea and preliminary rough sketches, are quite loose, most clients are unable to visualize how the printed piece will look. Consequently a much tighter version of the layout is required. This tighter layout is called a semi-comprehensive and is usually rendered on layout paper with Magic Markers.

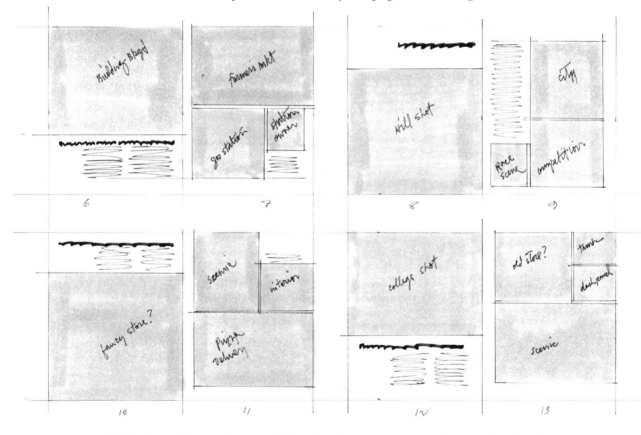

STEP 1. First I did a small-scale, 6¼″ x 4″ (16 x 10 cm), basic organizational layout as an aid in determining what the picture sizes would be on the pages. The proportions of this small rough are the same as those of the final larger size. Here I didn't attempt to render the illustrations; I just put a gray marker tone into the picture areas. I did, however, make notations about the subject matter in these areas to remind me of what the client would like to see used in the backgrounds. In the larger picture, a building was to be used, and the smaller ones would have a farmer's market, a gas station, and a small shot of a gas station attendant. Note that even the headline and copy blocks have been indicated in this rough.

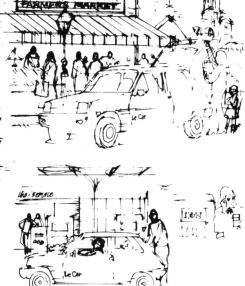

STEP 2. Next I did a full-size preliminary rough, 17″ x 11″ (43 x 28 cm), with black and gray markers on tracing paper. This rough layout was very important, as I was determining the exact sizes and views of the vehicles as well as the background situations. Even though these are roughly drawn, the illustrations are fairly accurate and the background scenes are quite clear. Shadow areas have been indicated to help clarify the illustrations better. This rough was to serve as my guide for rendering the semi-comprehensive layout.

STEP 3. Before proceeding to the comprehensive layout, I first had to do an accurate underlay drawing which would be used as a guide for drawing the cars and background scenes. I did this drawing using reference photographs whenever possible, especially for the vehicles, which had to be very accurate. I projected the photos of the cars to the correct size and traced them roughly with a Pentel pen. Then I sketched the backgrounds to complete the underlay drawing.

STEP-BY-STEP DEMONSTRATIONS

There's Something Practical About Owning a Le Car

Nobody builds cars quite like Renault. And no other small car is quite like Le Car. It zips through traffic with remarkable ease, and takes to the highway like a luxury sedan. It's more than just "transportation." It's a joy.

On the outside, Le Car features a stylish new grille. Rectangular headlights light up your way. And new fiberglass bumpers absorb the hard knocks of life. Inside, you'll find some of the changes we've made rather comforting. Like dual-spring, biomechanically engineered seats that maximize comfort and reduce driving fatigue. A new instrument panel that safely positions all controls and switches at your fingertips. And a more efficient heating and defogging system that's bound to keep the windows (and your toes) frost-free.

Whether it's cross town to work or cross country to play, Le Car is an immensely practical machine. It amazingly squeezes every last mile out of a gallon of gas, delivering an EPA-estimated mpg of 40 and a highway estimate of 46.

Renault Le Car. A pure driving pleasure. Distinctively French. Definitely "class." The kind of car that'll make the Joneses want to keep up with you.

STEP 4 (left). Next I positioned the previous drawing, the underlay sheet, under a sheet of layout paper, and traced it with a fine technical pen. Then I filled in this outline drawing with colored Magic Markers. It is best to build up your colors—that is, to begin by first putting in the lighter colors and then adding the darker ones, building these tones rather slowly. This is the right-hand page of the spread. I handled all the other pages in the catalog in exactly the same manner. These renderings were done on separate sheets of layout paper and then cut out accurately with an X-acto knife and mounted in position, using spray adhesive. The completed catalog, with all of the pages done in this manner, was then presented to the client for approval.

STEP 5 (above). The layout was approved, and so a photographer, Tim Doyle, was hired to shoot the photographs at suitable locations based on the illustrations in the layout. You can see how closely the layout was followed, although there was a change in the car's direction in the farmer's market scene.

SEMI-COMPREHENSIVE LAYOUT
MAGAZINE AD, AIR LANKA

This demonstration is of the development of a semi-comprehensive layout for a proposed ad for Air Lanka. In designing this magazine ad, I wanted to achieve a strong design layout and yet show the great variety found in Sri Lanka, the interesting people, the elephants, the unusual architecture, and the beautiful lakes. This demonstration is a good example of why it is so important to research your assignments properly—for, even though you might be dealing with unfamiliar subjects, your client probably knows them very well.

STEP 1. I began, as usual, by doing several preliminary roughs which helped me to determine the design of the ad. As rough as these layouts are, the picture content and the design are quite clear. The first two layouts are fairly standard, with a large picture area at the top and the copy block below. I wanted to do a more unusual ad, however, and I was more inclined to favor the layout with the elephant at the top, two pictures at the sides, and the large figure at the bottom. I also felt that this format, being a little unorthodox, would stand out among the other ads in a publication. The fact that the four pictures were separated and not in a group also appealed to me.

STEP 2. Next I worked up a tight underlay drawing, using a Pilot Razor Point pen on layout paper. To do this, I used visual references from various magazines and travel folders.

STEP 3. I positioned the underlay drawing under a sheet of layout paper and then rendered the man and the elephant in line with the Pilot pen. The gray tones were added next, using Magic Markers. I rendered these tones rather quickly, using bold strokes to retain a fresh look.

STEP-BY-STEP DEMONSTRATIONS

Sri Lanka

AIRLANKA

STEP 4 (above). I laid another sheet of layout paper over the rectangular pictures and went through exactly the same procedure for them, first doing the outline drawings with the Pilot pen and then rendering the gray tones.

STEP 5 (right). I added the headline, logo, and type indications next. This was done with a Pentel Sign Pen. I ruled in the body copy carefully with a technical pen.

Our Paradise

Sri Lanka   AIRLANKA

STEP 6 (left). I sprayed the two rectangular picture renderings on the back side with a spray cement, and then I carefully cut them out with an X-acto knife.

STEP 7 (right). Then I carefully mounted the cut-out renderings in position on the layout, completing the ad. Semi-comprehensive renderings are sufficient for most layouts, as they will show the subject matter and general effect quite clearly. If it had been desirable to present a much tighter layout for this assignment, I would have had type set or used Letraset and mounted the type in position in the layout.

SEMI-COMPREHENSIVE LAYOUT
MAGAZINE AD, LE CREUSET

I did this semi-comprehensive layout for a magazine ad for Le Creuset, a French kitchenware manufacturer. I was not involved in the design of the ad—I was only asked to do the rendering of the illustration. The client requested me to submit a pencil sketch of the situation before doing the actual layout rendering. In this case, I was actually given the product and was able to photograph it in the exact position I wanted, thereby solving a difficult drawing problem and saving time.

STEP 1. First I took a Polaroid photograph of the product. This simplified things a bit, as it saved me time when it came to drawing the object. When you work under tight deadlines, having the right photograph can be quite important. The photograph was blown up quickly with a Beseler projector, and then I drew the images roughly on tracing paper. I didn't really need a tight, accurate drawing at this stage—just one with the correct proportions. My first rough diagram/sketch, which was done with a soft 2B graphite pencil, established the basic composition.

STEP 2. I changed the composition slightly and then did a tighter pencil sketch, which was to be shown to Art Director Claude Louis of Impact/FCB for approval. The art director requested that I change the position of the tray below the pot so that the handles could be seen better.

STEP 3. Here is my revised pencil underlay drawing, which I used to do the final layout rendering.

STEP-BY-STEP DEMONSTRATIONS

STEP 5. I began the rendering by starting with the lighter tones and then putting in the dark background gray. I added shadows and details to the flowers, the floral design on the pot, and the disk in the lower right corner.

STEP 4. I positioned my underlay drawing beneath a sheet of layout paper and then drew all of the objects in outline form. I used a gray marker to draw the flowers in order to keep the effect softer.

STEP 6. I finished the rendering and then used a light gray Prismacolor pencil to draw in the pattern on the tablecloth. Prismacolor pencils, both the colored ones and the grays, are very compatible for use in conjunction with markers or even with paint. This completed rendering was then mounted onto the art director's layout and presented to the client along with several other ads.

COMPREHENSIVE LAYOUT, MARKERS
MAGAZINE AD, CANON

This assignment was for a black-and-white magazine ad for Canon. I was only involved with rendering the picture, as the ad had been designed by the art director, Jacques David of Impact/FCB, Paris. Ads for mechanical products like this one are fairly complex, as the drawings must be accurate. The use of circle and oval templates can greatly simplify some of the drawing problems. I was fortunate in having the client furnish me with the actual product, and this enabled me to take a few Polaroid photographs of it from the proper viewpoint.

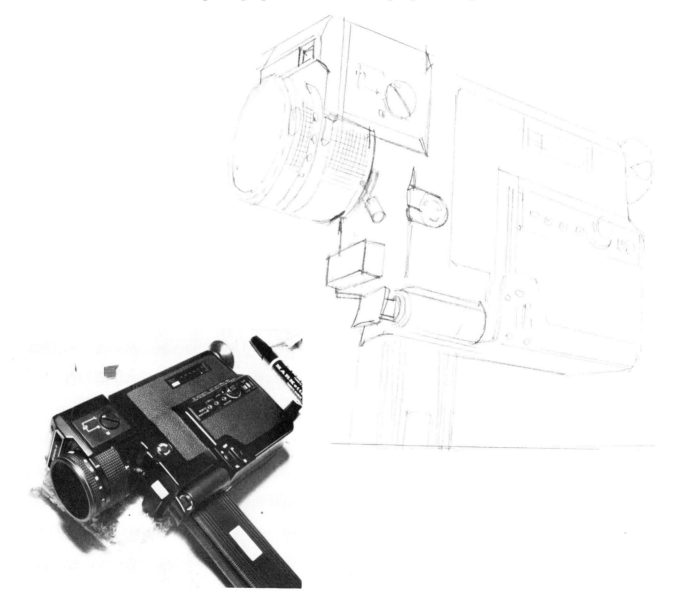

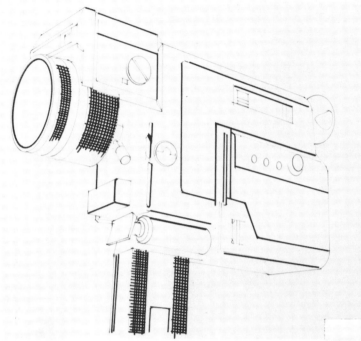

STEP 2. To trace the underlay drawing on the layout paper, I used a Pilot Razor Point pen for the finer lines and a Pentel Sign Pen for the heavier accented lines. The straight lines were drawn by using the edge of a triangle as a guide, and the ovals were done with oval guides.

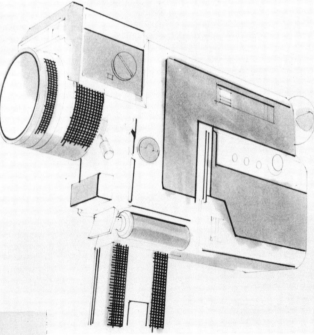

STEP 3. I began the rendering by first adding a very light gray overall background with a no. 1 gray Magic Marker. I did this rather quickly to keep the tone fresh-looking. If you work with markers too slowly when rendering large areas, the result will be an overlapping of tones rather than a smooth effect. Next I added the necessary gray tones to the camera.

STEP 4. Next I put the black areas in, as well as an intermediate gray to simulate a leatherlike texture. The final touch was the addition of white accents, which I painted in with permanent white designers' gouache using a no. 3 red sable watercolor brush.

COMPREHENSIVE LAYOUT, MARKERS
MAGAZINE AD, ROBOT MINUTE

This comprehensive layout was also for an ad for a mechanical product. I had to design the ad as well as do the rendering and lettering. My objective was to create a very strong, simple ad for this food-processing machine. It wasn't necessary to show the whole machine in the ad, but three cutting blades did have to be added.

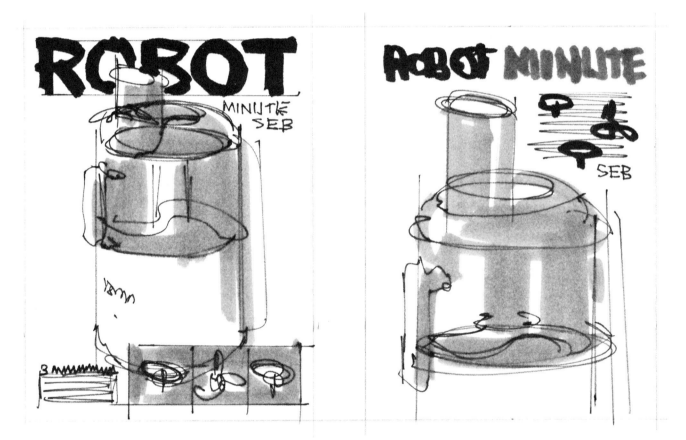

STEP 1. I began by working up miniature idea-rough sketches to establish the direction of the design. I preferred the sketch on the right, in which only the top portion of the machine is showing, as the image is stronger. I thought that I might be able to show the accessory blades spotted within the copy block.

STEP 2. I felt that a black background might work well, and so I did another sketch with this idea. It worked very well, and I decided to base the comprehensive layout on this approach.

STEP 3. Having a photograph of the exact view of the product simplified matters, as I could project the image to the correct size with my Beseler projector. Then I traced the image roughly on layout paper with an HB graphite pencil. This rough drawing would serve as the underlay guide for the final rendering.

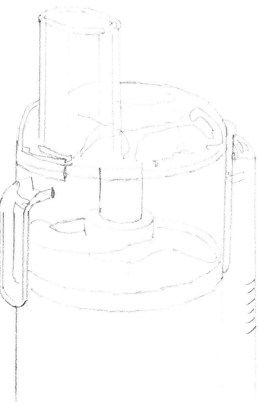

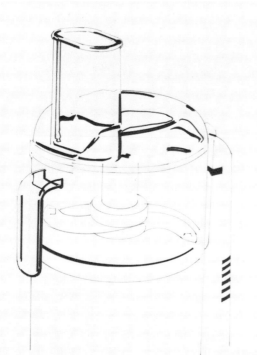

STEP 4 (above, left). Using my previous drawing as an underlay, I traced the outlines and details of the product on layout paper with a Pilot pen. I drew in the heavier lines and accents with a Pentel Sign Pen.

STEP 5 (above, right). With nos. 2, 5, 7, and 9 gray Magic Markers I boldly blocked in the tones on the Robot machine, following my photograph as a guide for the values. Then I added black accents in the appropriate areas.

STEP 6 (right). Next I put a black tone over the whole background, working quickly to keep the tone even and smooth. Then I added the highlights and reflections with a gray Prismacolor pencil. I completed the rendering by painting in the stronger highlights with white paint.

STEP 7. I drew the lettering on a sheet of layout paper, tracing this directly onto the black background. I rubbed a tone of light gray Prismacolor pencil behind the letters so an image would transfer onto the background when traced. The letters and the small spot drawings were painted with white paint and a small sable brush.

COMPREHENSIVE LAYOUT, MARKERS
MAGAZINE AD, LANCÔME

Many ads for beauty products show a large picture of the product it-self, and usually these products are in containers that look like many other packages. I wanted to minimize the actual product container and box, concentrating the major visual image on the result of the product—in this case, lipstick. This comprehensive magazine ad lay-out was done using pencils with the markers. Often, marker layouts can be tightened up and small details added by using pencils. Also, marker tones that are not perfectly flat frequently can be smoothed out with pencils.

STEP 1. First I did a few idea doodles with a black Design Art Marker and a no. 5 gray for the tones. A couple of these sketches were inter-esting, and I decided to develop them a bit further. The sketch at the top was an unusual layout approach which could work, but I really liked the versions with the very large face.

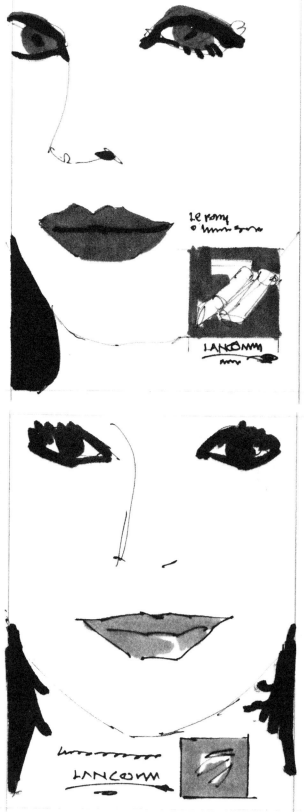

STEP 2. Next I did slightly larger interpretations in the form of idea-rough sketches; these layouts were more detailed and finished. I felt that the design that worked best was the one with the large head facing directly out of the page. This seemed to be the strongest design, for it emphasized the lips, the most important part of the ad.

STEP 3. Using a couple of photographs from magazines for reference, I did an underlay drawing on a sheet of layout paper. (I also could have taken a Polaroid photograph of a model for the reference.) In addition, I indicated on this underlay where the lettering would appear and did a rough sketch of the product for the minor illustration.

STEP 4. I positioned a sheet of layout paper over the underlay drawing and started to render the head very simply in a very light no. 2 gray Magic Marker. The subtle shading and modeling of the face was accomplished with medium gray and black Prismacolor pencils. It is very difficult to blend marker tones smoothly, as hard edges usually result when they are used over other tones. By far the best method is using pencils for blending, especially the wax type such as Prismacolor. I used a black marker to draw in the hair and eyelashes.

Le rouge a lèvres satin.....

LANCÔME

PARIS

STEP 5. I rendered the product illustration on a separate sheet of layout paper and then cut it out carefully with an X-acto knife and mounted it into position. Then I put in the lettering and trademark with a Pentel Sign Pen, completing the ad.

73

STEP-BY-STEP DEMONSTRATIONS

COMPREHENSIVE LAYOUT,
MARKERS
MAGAZINE AD, BRITISH AEROSPACE

I wanted to achieve a very strong poster effect in my layout for this proposed ad for British Aerospace. I simulated a high-contrast dropout photograph of the aircraft which would later be used in the finished ad. A high-contrast photograph is one in which all of the intermediate grays have been eliminated, leaving only a stark black-and-white image. I felt that the strong graphic effect achieved through this method would create an interesting, effective ad.

STEP 1. First I did a couple of small idea-rough sketches to establish the angle of the aircraft. The sketch on the right, the one with the aircraft in a steep dive, worked the best. The ad needed to show the aircraft at an extreme angle to catch the reader's eye.

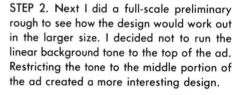

STEP 2. Next I did a full-scale preliminary rough to see how the design would work out in the larger size. I decided not to run the linear background tone to the top of the ad. Restricting the tone to the middle portion of the ad created a more interesting design.

STEP 3. The next step was to do the tissue underlay drawing by projecting a photograph of the aircraft to the exact size wanted, then tracing the image on layout paper. This was drawn with a Design Art Marker.

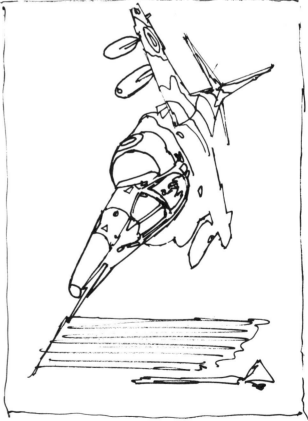

STEP 4. Next I traced the underlay drawing onto another sheet of layout paper, using a technical pen for the outline.

STEP 5. I began to outline all of the black areas carefully with a Pentel Sign Pen. This was done so I could fill in the black areas more easily.

STEP 6. The drawing was completed by filling in all of the black areas with a Pentel pen. The Pentel produces a smooth, even black tone that is more uniform than the tone produced by a black marker.

The design, development, production and assembly lines of British Aerospace are meeting defence requirements which are unequalled in their breadth and variety. Alone or in collaboration with industry leaders in other countries, British Aerospace Aircraft Group provides the solution to military needs which include basic and advanced pilot, aircrew and weapons training . . . military transport and in-flight refuelling . . . coastal patrol and long-range maritime surveillance . . . subsonic ground attack and supersonic tactical strike and reconnaissance . . . VSTOL and carrier-borne combat operations . . . Mach 2-plus, all-weather air defence and ultra-low-level strike. Missile systems designed, developed and manufactured by British Aerospace Dynamics Group are providing Great Britain and many overseas nations with cost-effective defence against ultra-low-level attack by supersonic aircraft . . . against missile and aircraft attacks on naval forces . . . against armoured attack on land . . . and against hostile aircraft in close-combat and long-range interception operations.

BRITISH AEROSPACE
unequalled in its range of aerospace programmes
British Aerospace Public Limited Company, Weybridge, England.

STEP 7. Finally I added the lines over the aircraft by using a Letratone dry transfer sheet no. LT 67. Letraset sheets are available with many different designs and patterns which can be used over artwork or on layouts. Then I mounted the type and logo onto the layout. The letters GRMK 3 were done with Letraset Instant Lettering, using 72-point Compacta bold italic type.

PAINTED COMPREHENSIVE LAYOUT
MAGAZINE AD FOR BMW

When I designed this ad, I was after a strong visual image—something that would stand out in a publication. Many automotive ads are done using photographs with backgrounds, and I felt that by silhouetting the image against a white background I could make this ad more distinctive. This demonstration is of a painted comprehensive layout in which I used washes of water-soluble ink on illustration board. To do a layout like this properly, you must have very good reference material so the product will be accurately portrayed. Good reference material helps not only with various details, but also with the lighting of the product.

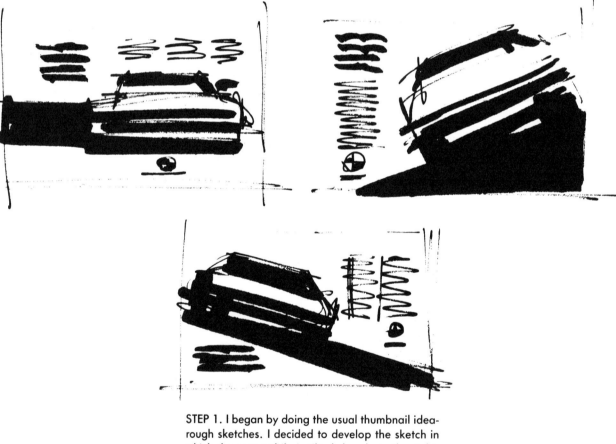

STEP 1. I began by doing the usual thumbnail idea-rough sketches. I decided to develop the sketch in which the automobile is tilted sharply to the right, thereby creating an interesting long shadow across the page. The angle of the automobile and the long shadow lead the viewer's eye right into the ad.

why people
who own a BMW
enjoy driving more
than you do.

STEP 2 (above). I was very pleased with the effect, as it created a very dramatic ad design. I decided to proceed with this format.

STEP 3 (right). I did a pencil drawing on illustration board, drawing it directly from a projected image of a photograph of the vehicle. Next, I inked the drawing with a technical pen, using a French curve and triangle as guides for some of the lines.

STEP 4 (above). I began painting the vehicle by washing a tone of gray over the
hood and the windshield. The wash was
a tone of diluted water-soluble ink. I
added a darker wash tone to the side of
the car and under the bumper. I dried
these washes very quickly with a hair-
dryer. I used a no. 6 red sable watercolor brush for painting the washes.

STEP 5 (right). Next I painted a few reflections as well as the dark interior, and
then I darkened the area underneath the
bumper further with an additional dark
wash of ink. I painted these smaller details with a no. 4 red sable brush, as it
was easier to work on these areas with
the smaller brush.

STEP 6 (left). I wanted a very deep, black tone in the shadow under the vehicle, and so I painted this in with ivory black designers' gouache. The highlights on the chrome parking lights and headlights were painted in with permanent white designers' gouache.

STEP 7 (below). Last of all I added the type, which had been set; the logo; and the headline, for which I used Letraset Instant Lettering.

The BMW owner comes in a far wider variety than the BMW.

Presidents, diplomats, princes, dukes, senators, astronauts, doctors, judges, captains of industries, motion picture stars, directors, merchants, accountants and business executives of all types and varieties.

Diverse as BMW owners may be, however, virtually all have one thing in common: a glassy-eyed, unabashed affection for their car. An affection that paradoxically seems to increase as the years and miles go by.

What makes the BMW 733i so different from other cars?

There is an obsolescence built into most cars – even the most costly – that has nothing to do with the way they're constructed.

It's called boredom. And it has to do with the way they drive.

Most cars simply are not built to perform in such a way that driving becomes an end – not merely an uninspired means of transporting oneself from one place to another.

The BMW 733i, on the other hand, is.

"The reaction to a BMW is always the same," writes an editor of Motor Trend magazine. "The first time driver takes the wheel and after a few miles no other automobile like this will ever be quite as good again."

A car that's engineered, not styled.

Perhaps the engineers at the Bavarian Motor Works did not coin the phrase, form follows function, "But," say the editors of Motor Trend, "among the world's automakers BMW is perhaps the foremost practitioner of that philosophy."

The ultimate driving machine

Why people who own a BMW enjoy driving more than you do.

TV STORYBOARDS
TV SPOT FOR LE CREUSET

The problems involved in doing TV storyboards are different from those of an ad or a poster. The main difference is that the artist must produce a greater number of individual pieces, and usually, they must be done under more harried conditions than most other assignments. The style of rendering shown in this demonstration is one I have developed over a number of years and which is widely accepted by many clients. I developed the technique so that I could produce a great many TV storyboard renderings in a short span of time. It is a simple, direct method, well-suited for producing fresh-looking renderings. This assignment was done for Jean-René Ruttinger, Director of the Radio, Cinema, and Television Department of Impact/FCB, Paris.

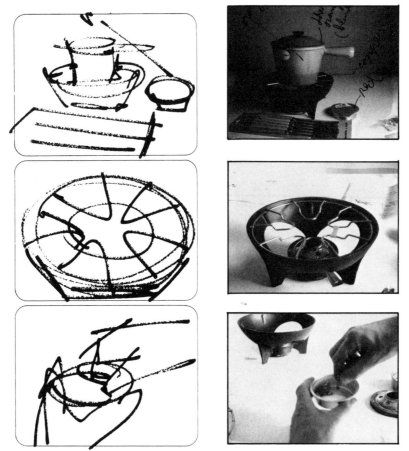

STEP 1. I did these idea sketches in the TV producer's office while he was briefing me on the assignment. Sketches such as these help to clarify product views, angles of the scenes, size of objects, and what emphasis is to be placed on the various elements. Since there are usually many frames in a film, more information must be remembered by the layout artist, and sketches like these are invaluable.

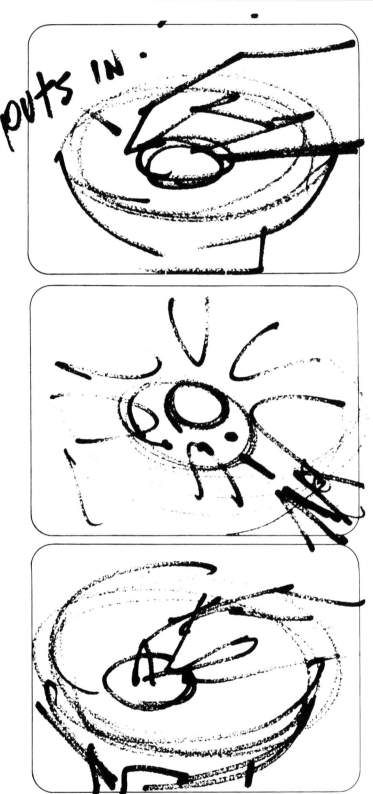

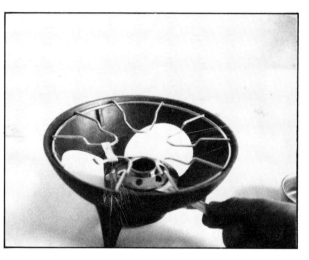

STEP 2. I was given the product, a fondue pot and heater, which greatly simplified my assignment and shortened the drawing time, since I could photograph the product in the exact angle requested and then project the image to the correct size. These photographs were taken with a Polaroid camera. The quality of reference photographs is not important, as long as the views of the objects are correct.

STEP 3. I projected the photographs to size and then drew the images on tracing paper with an HB graphite pencil. These drawings would be used as underlays for doing the final renderings.

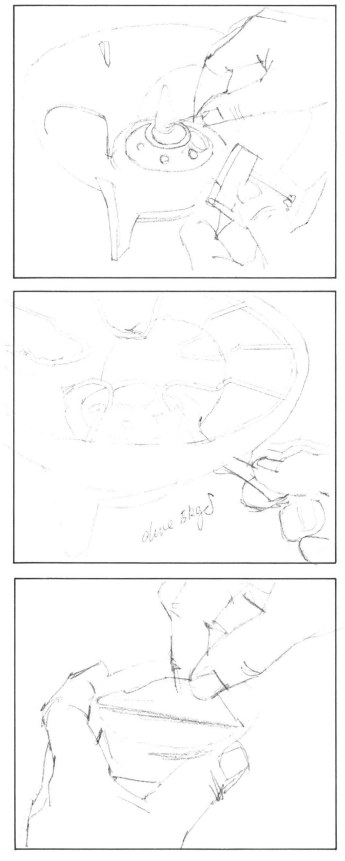

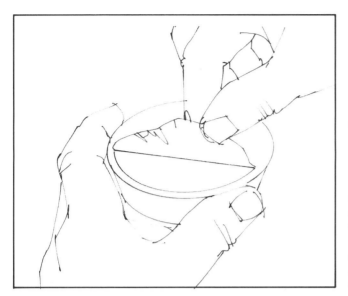

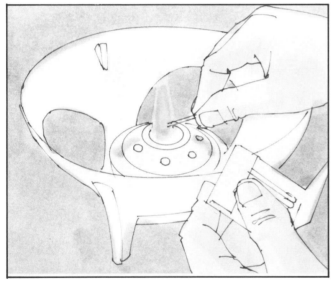

STEP 4. I traced the underdrawings on a sheet of layout paper with a Pilot pen. I drew all of the frames in the story-board in this manner before starting to add color.

STEP 5. To color the images, I began by adding tone to the background. Incidentally, I should mention here that in order to speed things up, I quickly rendered all of the back-grounds at the same time. Then I went back to the first frame and put in the flame, the flesh tone, and a simple shadow tone on the hands.

STEP 6. I added a dark tone to the fondue pot holder, some color to the heating unit, and a few appropriate shadows and accents, finishing the frame. The whole operation took only a matter of minutes once my basic drawing was fin-ished; that's why this is a perfect technique for doing a great number of frames in a very short time. The basic line drawing is really what holds the whole picture together, and the subsequent color tones can be put on rather freely, creating a very fresh effect.

PART 4

TYPICAL ASSIGNMENTS

The purpose of this section is to examine twelve different assignments, from conception right through to final comprehensive layout—or, whenever possible, the finished, printed piece. The range of assignments shown will give you a better idea of the diversity of the projects with which a layout artist must cope on a daily (and sometimes nightly) basis. The assignments include newspaper and magazine ads, posters, catalogs, booklets, brochure covers, and TV storyboards. The subject matter involved is also quite diverse, covering a broad spectrum of products in advertising. The great variety of assignments and products an artist becomes involved with is one of the more interesting aspects of the business. Some artists, however, do specialize in specific areas such as automotive or fashion advertising—but this is the exception, rather than the normal method of working.

You will notice that in some of the assignments, I was not required to go through all of the possible layout stages; in some cases I went from preliminary rough sketch directly to the finished art. In other instances, I went from preliminary rough sketch right to the comprehensive layout, without doing the intermediate semi-comprehensive layout. Actually, there is no set sequence of stages required to produce an assignment; it depends on the artist and the client. You may feel that you want to do a semi-comprehensive layout, even if it is not required, just to be sure that the work is developing properly. If your client has difficulties visualizing ideas, he or she might require that you progress through every possible stage of layout development, including a tight painted comprehensive. Time and money also play a definite role in the process, and sometimes most of the layout phases may be eliminated because of budget or deadline problems.

Doing layout renderings is not an easy job, as a great deal is required of the artist. The artist must be able to draw fairly well, work out a composition, and render a wide variety of subject matter. It is mandatory that the layout artist be able to simulate various art and photographic techniques. A layout artist has an advantage if he or she possesses a creative flair and is aware of the current trends in the business. All of these factors combine to make advertising layout an interesting and challenging business, as you will see on the following pages. The assignments shown will show you a good cross section of the variety of work with which an advertising designer and layout-rendering artist is involved.

NEWSPAPER AD SERIES FOR THE AMERICAN COLLEGE IN PARIS

The objective of this assignment was to create a series of newspaper ads to promote the college and create interest among potential students, who could obtain additional information about the school by sending for a catalog. One ad was to be a general one, and the other two were to be devoted specifically to European Cultural Studies and French Studies. The ads were to be designed so that they retained a family resemblance and would reproduce well in newspapers. I decided to use line art rather than photographs in the finished ads, as artwork would reproduce much better on the coarse newsprint paper. Since most pictures and ads in the newspapers are photographs, I also felt that artwork would stand out more. The ads would be tied together through consistency of design, typography, and the style of illustration.

IDEA ROUGH. This was one of my first idea roughs, which I made after deciding what subjects should be illustrated in the ads. This ad is promoting European Cultural Studies, and since I wanted to show a group of students studying on location at an easily recognizable landmark in Paris, I decided on Notre Dame Cathedral.

PRELIMINARY ROUGH SKETCH. The next step was to find reference material on Notre Dame Cathedral and a group of students. I checked through my own photographic reference file and found a few photos which would work well. From this material, I was able to do this preliminary rough sketch. Here, I have carried the design concept a little further to establish the basic layout of the ad. This preliminary rough was to be used as a guide when I worked up the comprehensive ad. A sketch such as this is also finished enough to be presented when discussing ideas with the client.

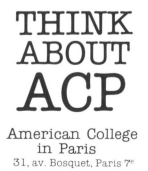

Think about
EUROPEAN CULTURAL STUDIES

Think about Europe. There is no better place to study European Culture than in Europe; especially in Paris where the past and present have merged into a fascinating, if sometimes perplexing, whole. The B.A. Program in European Cultural Studies at the American College in Paris analyzes European Culture from a variety of perspectives. The disciplines of Art History, European Literature and History are studied as the core elements making up the cultural heritage of Europe today. Students interpret the significance of these elements in relation to the historical periods that produced them. Ultimately the European Cultural Studies major acquires the critical tools to assess and appreciate cultural phenomena in general.

The European Cultural Studies Program takes a challenging approach to achieve an interdisciplinary view of human history. It is particularly well-suited to students who need a solid but diverse background as part of their training in law, education, library science, or journalism, or for advanced study in the humanities.

European Cultural Studies at ACP. Think about it.

THINK ABOUT ACP

American College in Paris
31, av. Bosquet, Paris 7ᵉ

COMPREHENSIVE LAYOUT. Here is the finished tight comprehensive layout with the headline and body copy mounted in place. I decided to do a really tight presentation layout so that the art technique would be very clear to the client. The best way to accomplish this was to draw the actual finished artwork and mount a photostat or other copy of it in place on the layout for presentation. The illustration was done by drawing with an ultra-fine-line Design Art Marker for the thin lines and a Markette Thinrite marker for the textural tones. It was drawn on a rough watercolor paper so that the surface could be utilized to create textural interest.

IDEA ROUGH. This idea rough was made for a general ad promoting ACP, and in this case, I decided to use an illustration of the college entrance with a few students milling around. The idea rough was not intended for presentation to the client; it was only for my own evaluation, a necessary step in designing the ad.

PRELIMINARY ROUGH SKETCH. This sketch for the second ad was done for myself, so I could better visualize the design of the ad. Note how a rough sketch like this can help to clarify problems such as the shape of the illustration, the position of the type and headline, and the spotting of the black accents in the illustration.

THINK
ABOUT
ACP

Think about Paris. For centuries the city of Paris has been a center of Western culture and offers extraordinary opportunities for the study of the history of art. The city as a museum and the museums within the city—and Europe itself—serve as an unequalled resource for a student of art history. Not only are the Louvre, the Centre Georges Pompidou and the Jeu de Paume invaluable, but the student can visit the little-known and the private museums in Paris, and can travel with faculty members on conducted field trips to Italy, Greece, Holland, England and elsewhere. This direct confrontation with works of art in their geographical, historical and cultural environment is the most challenging aspect of ACP's Art History Program. In this B.A. program, every major period of Western art is studied with emphasis on European Art. Introductory courses equip the student to identify and analyze works of art. Advanced courses are period and genre oriented, and additional courses in studio arts, cultural studies and a wide choice of languages permit an interdisciplinary approach to the study of the history of art.

American College in Paris
31, av Bosquet, Paris 7ᵉ France

COMPREHENSIVE LAYOUT. This finished tight comprehensive layout is ready for presentation. The headline and body copy were typeset and mounted in the layout, as was a photocopy of the artwork, which had been done in the same manner as the illustrations in the other ad. I had taken a quick Polaroid photo of the college entrance and used this and other photos for reference in doing the artwork. Taking Polaroid photographs is the quickest and surest method of obtaining necessary reference material.

PRELIMINARY ROUGH SKETCH. This was done for another, slightly larger newspaper ad for ACP, focusing on French Studies. It wasn't necessary to do an idea rough for this ad, as I had already established the basic layout concept through the other ads. I had a few photographs of the Pont Neuf bridge and felt that it would make an interesting, recognizable image for this ad. Notice how the design of the illustration leads the reader's eye right into the copy block.

Think about FRENCH STUDIES

Think about France and the French. A full understanding of French culture is the primary aim of the B.A. Program in French Studies at the American College in Paris through a broad selection of courses in language and literature. The French Studies major concentrates on proficiency in spoken and written French, skills which are further developed by life in Paris—shopping in the open markets, reading the French-language newspapers, having breakfast in a café. Numerous trips conducted by the faculty in Paris and throughout France give the student first-hand knowledge of areas of importance in the development of the French culture. ACP's Cultural Program Office obtains reduced rate tickets for theatre, music and dance events which often parallel the classroom study. With the approval of an academic advisor, a French Studies major may enroll in courses in language and literature at the University of Paris.

At the American College in Paris, the student has the distinct advantage of being able to earn a B.A. degree in French Studies, in the ideal location . . . France.

French Studies at ACP. Think about it.

THINK ABOUT ACP

American College in Paris

COMPREHENSIVE LAYOUT. The finished comprehensive layout was done in exactly the same way as the others in this series. I felt that the overall concept, the artwork, and the individual ad designs combined well to create an effective campaign. This proposed ad campaign did not develop into finished ads, but had the campaign been accepted, it would have been a simple procedure to complete the ads for printing, since the artwork was already finished.

MAGAZINE ADS FOR POSTER CAMPAIGN, CARTE BLEUE / VISA

In this assignment I was involved only in rendering the pictorial material for the campaign. It was a difficult assignment, as a total of nine comprehensive layouts had to be done in five days. The layouts also were rather large, the subject matter was fairly complex, and everything had to be completed over a weekend. I managed to finish everything on time, but four of the ads had to be redone, as the art director was not happy with what I had done. I finished the new layouts in two days, and they were accepted by the art director and mounted into the layouts with type and body copy for presentation to the client.

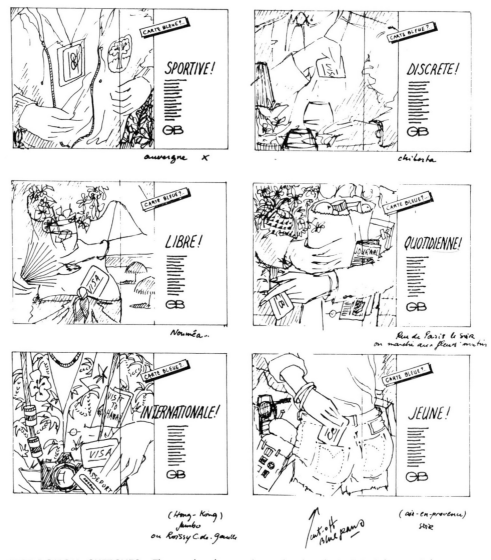

IDEA-ROUGH SKETCHES. These sketches were done by Jacques Despoix, the art director for this series of ads. They are small in scale and quite loose, but nevertheless they show clearly what pictorial material was to be shown in the ads. He discussed each ad with me so that there would be no confusion about what should be done.

IDEA-ROUGH SKETCH. Some of the roughs were done on a larger scale, and this is one that I used as a guide for producing my comprehensive rendering. Many art directors just explain an assignment, but it is a great help if they also do a simple diagrammatic sketch of just what they have in mind. In this case, the art director decided against showing the other aircraft in the window; it would have been not only impossible to photograph, but also unlikely that two aircraft would be so dangerously close.

UNDERLAY DRAWING. This rough pencil drawing was used as the underlay for producing the comprehensive layout. It was drawn on tracing paper with a 2B graphite pencil. I found reference material for the window in a travel magazine. You might think that you can remember or guess what a certain object looks like, but it is much better to try to find suitable visual references to be sure. Note that even though this drawing was done rather roughly, all of the proportions are accurate and everything has been composed carefully.

COMPREHENSIVE LAYOUT. Reproduced here is the finished comprehensive layout, complete with type, headline, and logo. I began this rendering by tracing my previous underlay drawing in line and then putting in the lighter colors and tones with Magic Markers. I built up the darker colors and tones gradually until the illustration was completed. I am always very careful not to overwork marker tones so that my rendering will retain a fresh, clean look. The lettering on the airline ticket was done with Prismacolor pencils; this is a good method for adding smaller details that would be too difficult to render with markers. The white lettering, highlights, and reflections were done with designers' gouache.

FINISHED AD. This is the magazine ad as it appeared in print. It is basically the same as the comprehensive layout, but a few minor alterations have been made. The photographs for this series were done by Gerard Mongalvy, a Paris-based photographer.

UNDERLAY DRAWING (below). This pencil underlay drawing was developed from the art director's rough sketch and was drawn on a sheet of layout paper with an HB graphite pencil. Rather than try to draw these items from memory, I worked from Polaroid photos and pictures in cookbooks. The photos were all projected to size with a Beseler projector and then traced roughly with a pencil.

IDEA-ROUGH SKETCH (right). The posters in this campaign were to be companion pieces to the ads and had to be done with the same basic format and feeling. Often the artist is asked to relate various pieces of advertising material in this way when producing layouts for a large campaign. This is the art director's rough sketch for one of the posters. It measures 6½'' x 9'' (16 x 23 cm) and is done in the same proportions as the full-size final printed piece. This rough shows a kitchen scene with fish, crab, vegetables, and the Carte Bleue, suggesting that the person has just purchased these items with the handy card.

COMPREHENSIVE LAYOUT (above). I traced the underlay drawing onto a sheet of layout paper with a fine-line marker and drew some of the objects such as the fish, crab, and vegetables with a gray Prismacolor pencil. I did this because I wanted these items to have softer edges in the finished rendering. As is my usual practice, I added the color by first working with the lighter tones and then building up the darker ones slowly. I added Prismacolor pencil accents and shading to the mushrooms, pepper, carrots, and crab. I also drew in the scales with dark and medium gray Prismacolor pencils. The highlights on the fish, as well as the letters on the card, were painted in with white paint and a brush.

FINISHED POSTER (right). As shown in this finished version of the poster, the client decided he did not want the fish in the foreground, but otherwise the idea has remained basically the same.

IDEA-ROUGH SKETCH (right). This is the art director's rough sketch for another poster in the same series. It spells out clearly the items that must be shown and even gives a pretty good idea of how much emphasis should be given to the various objects.

UNDERLAY DRAWING (below). This drawing was done on layout paper with an HB graphite pencil and was based on the art director's sketch. I found most of the reference material for this drawing in magazine pictures. Again, this rather loose rendition was sufficient, as the proportions and placement are accurate. Notice that I changed the composition slightly, enlarging the sunglasses and flower and adding a palm leaf in the upper right-hand corner. I also altered the perspective on the Visa card to make it more prominent.

BLEU AZUR

GB
*ELLE VOUS
SIMPLIFIE LA VIE !*

COMPREHENSIVE LAYOUT. This comp was done in the same manner as all of the others in this group—with Magic Markers on layout paper. I used Prismacolor pencils to shade the flowers and blend some of the tones on the glass. I used a dark blue Prismacolor pencil over the flower's leaves and on the palm frond in order to alter the marker tones in these areas.

FINISHED POSTER. The finished poster shows that the composition as shown in the comprehensive layout was altered somewhat: the sunglasses have been replaced by a snorkel mask, the flower has been moved, shells have been added, the color of the drink is now a strong yellow, and the shape of the glass is also different.

SIXTEEN-PAGE CATALOG FOR AMC / RENAULT LeCAR AND 18i

The objective of this assignment was to create powerful, distinctive cover designs for two separate catalogs while retaining a strong family resemblance between them. The products did not need to be shown on the covers if an interesting enough design concept could be developed. As far as the interior pages were concerned, I was to keep the design clean, simple, and flexible enough to allow for last-minute changes and additions. The client gave me all of the information as to what material was to be shown. Catalogs are much more complex than most advertising assignments because of the inherent problems of design continuity throughout a number of pages. I am often involved with catalog design and enjoy the challenge of such an assignment very much.

IDEA-ROUGH SKETCHES. A catalog is usually begun by starting with the cover design, which is probably the most important part of the catalog. I did one cover idea-rough sketch incorporating the product, but I felt that perhaps just the name of the automobiles, 18i and Le Car, would enable me to create more striking cover designs. Using lettering also would simplify the problem of tying the two catalogs together through design. After working out a couple of more roughs, shown here on the lower right, I decided that a silver background color should be used, with perhaps red and white letters. The real problem here would be to design the lettering properly so that an interesting, unusual design would be created.

PRELIMINARY ROUGHS. Next I did a few small preliminary rough sketches. The one on the left worked fairly well, but I decided that the lettering was not interesting enough. In my next rough, I squared off the 18i letters and made them bolder, as well as changing their color to dark gray, and the design started to take form. I worked up the Le Car cover rough, this time using red on the lettering, and I felt there was enough of a family resemblance to make the idea work. I showed these last two roughs to my client, and he was very pleased with the concept—especially the use of the silver as a background color.

COMPREHENSIVE LAYOUTS. I did not do Magic Marker comprehensive layouts for these cover designs, as my client decided to present very tight comps as close to the finished, printed piece as possible. We hired Dick Martini, a Detroit-based lettering artist, to develop the cover lettering based on my designs. These letters were then silk-screened directly onto the silver cover stock in red, gray, and white colors, producing very striking covers. This is an excellent method for producing extremely tight comprehensive layouts, especially when you are doing a design-oriented layout. For the finished covers, only a few minor alterations were made in the design: the words *American Motors* were moved up with Renault, and the year was added to each of the covers.

IDEA-ROUGH SKETCH. After I developed the cover designs, my next task was to work out the interior page designs of the catalogs. This is the idea-rough sketch for the opening spread, another important part of a catalog. I was to show a large beauty shot of the car and three smaller photographs of different car models in various situations.

PRELIMINARY ROUGH SKETCH. I liked the way the idea-rough sketch worked and decided to do a slightly more finished layout, this time in color, to see if this concept could be developed. This page-spread layout is quite important, as it is the key to the design of all the other pages in the book. When you are designing a catalog, the best method is to work out the pages completely on a small scale, as I did with this one, before beginning to do the full-size comprehensive layout. This way you can spread all of the layouts out on a table, study the design flow, and get an overview of the complete catalog. At this stage it is easy to determine whether any design alterations are necessary.

THE REMARKABLE
RENAULT 18i

COMPREHENSIVE LAYOUT (above). This is the comprehensive layout for the opening spread of the AMC/Renault 18i catalog. The letters and type were silk-screened onto a paper stock and the marker renderings were carefully cut out and mounted in place using a spray cement. These renderings are not quite as tight as most comps—they look more like semi-comprehensive layouts. When you are confronted with doing a great number of renderings, as for a catalog, you often have to do them a little looser to meet the deadline. The fact that the lettering is so tight helps give the overall impression of a much tighter layout. The renderings were all done on layout paper with fine-line marker pens for the outlines and Magic Markers for the color.

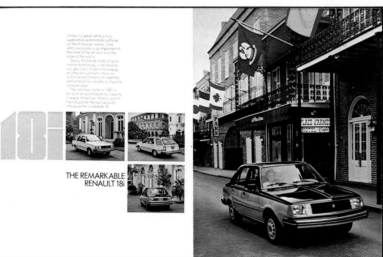

PRINTED CATALOG-PAGE SPREAD (right). You can see that the finished catalog spread is almost the same as the comprehensive layout. One change is the lighter gray lettering. The scene locations in the photographs also have changed.

ENGINEERING SPREAD, AMC/RENAULT LeCAR CATALOG

Often catalogs present the designer with difficult design problems, as frequently a great deal of information must be included on a page spread. In this assignment I had to show the AMC/Renault engineering story by including photos of the factory, manufacturing methods, quality control, testing of the cars, some important car details, and a cutaway engineering drawing of the automobile.

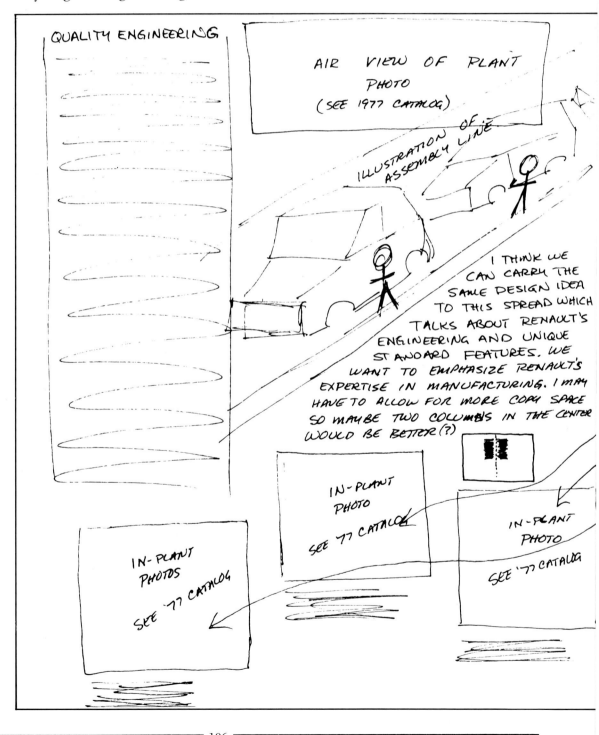

CLIENT'S IDEA-ROUGH SKETCH. My client made this rough sketch to show me what information was required on the engineering spread of the catalog. Client roughs like this, while they make no attempt at design, are nevertheless good graphic representations of the information that should be included, as well as the emphasis that the items should be given on the pages. Even an approximation of the amount of copy has been included.

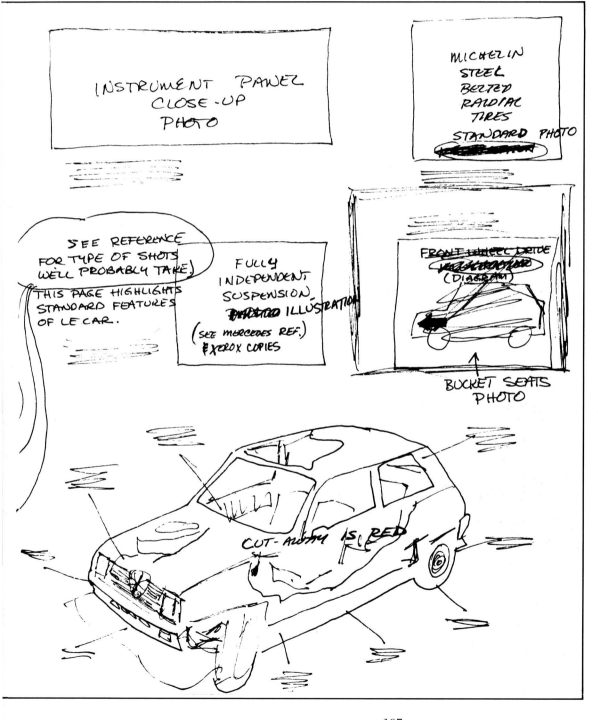

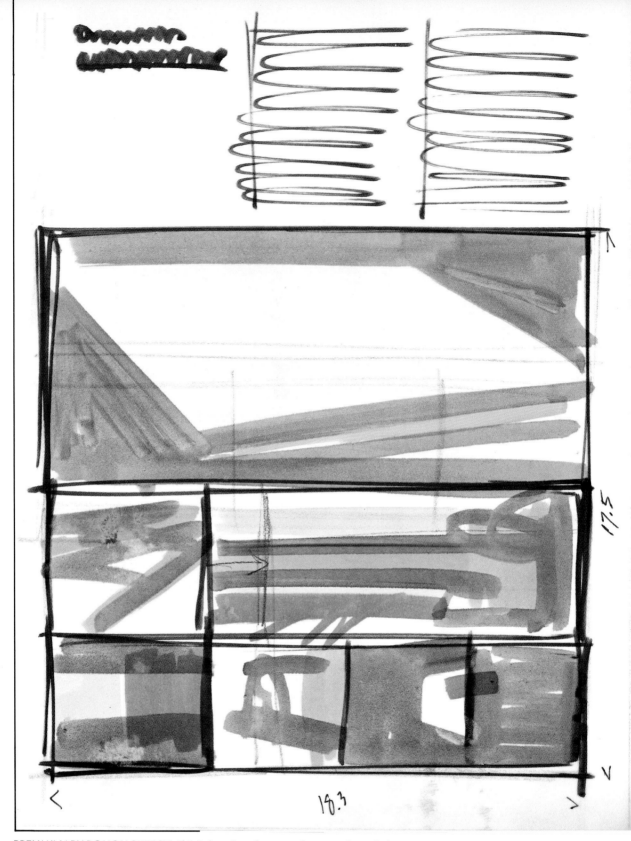

PRELIMINARY ROUGH SKETCH. This is how I envisioned the engineering spread. It was a problem not so much of design as of organization. I felt that keeping all of the elements in two equal boxes would simplify the problem greatly. In this way I could run the headline and body copy across the top of both pages. By emphasizing two elements, the factory photograph and the cutaway engineering drawing, I could make a more interesting design than if I were to make everything relatively the same size. This sketch was done on tracing paper with Magic Markers. You can see the importance of organizing each page thoroughly before proceeding with the comprehensive layout.

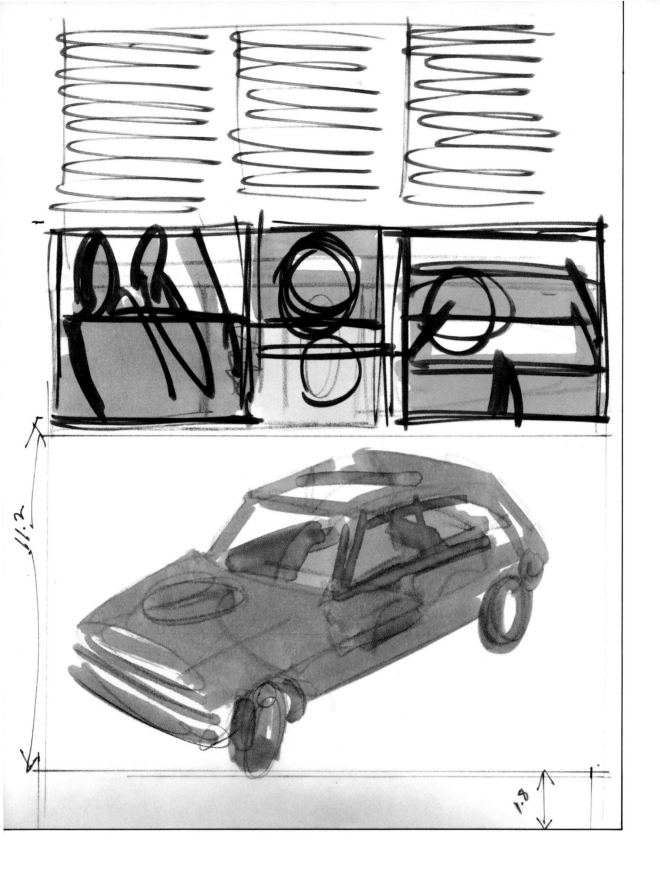

Quality Engineering

COMPREHENSIVE LAYOUT. Here is the finished layout as it was presented to American Motors. I used Letraset transfer type for the headlines and ruled in the copy blocks with a technical pen. I rendered the scenes by using other catalog photographs as reference material. I used a technical pen to draw the basic outlines on the illustrations and filled in the colors with Magic Markers. These renderings were all done separately, and then I cut them out accurately with an X-acto knife before mounting them on the layout.

TYPICAL ASSIGNMENTS

Flins, France...Home of Renault Le Car

Renault automobiles and parts are manufactured in eleven different plants in France, while another twenty-six assembly and manufacturing facilities are located throughout the world. As the leading French car builder, Renault produces a wide range of vehicles to supply the varied needs of the world, and almost 60% of its total production is exported to more than 150 countries.

The Pierre Lefaucheux plant, just 25 miles from Paris in Flins, France, is the home of Le Car and the Renault 18. This 585 acre man-ufacturing complex is considered to be one of the most modern and efficient factories in the world, employing more than 26,000 people. Each day, the plant produces an incredible 1,700 vehicles, chrome plates more than a quarter million parts of 500 different types and ships 330 tons of spare parts to dealers and importers worldwide. Renault's major vehicle delivery center is also headquartered at Flins and ships cars in trainloads (51% of the shipments), on specially equipped trucks (30%) and on barges on the Seine River (19%).

A. The Pierre Lefaucheux plant in Flins, France.
B. French craftsmanship and pride go hand-in-hand in building Le Car. C. After being degreased and chemically treated to prevent oxidation, car bodies are dipped in tank of anti-corrosion primer. D. Bodies are

inspected and hand finished prior to soundproofing and leakproofing. E. Special sealants are applied to fenders, quarter panels and wheel housings before assembly. F. Le Car is given a two-step paint application both inside and outside, including sealer spray. G. Over

1,500 quality control checks are made on Le Car during production including a test drive on a 3.8 km circuit which reproduces most road conditions you'll encounter. Adjustments are made prior to final shipment to dealers.

PRINTED CATALOG SPREAD. The printed piece follows the comprehensive layout pretty closely, but a headline has been added on the right-hand page.

ADVERTISING LAYOUT

European Engineering at Its Finest

Renault Le Car is a superior example of small car engineering, a standard of European automotive technology. To begin with, it features front wheel drive. And while front wheel drive is finally being hailed as the drivetrain arrangement of the future, it may interest you to know that Renault *pioneered* the development of front wheel drive when it first introduced the R-4 — *nineteen years ago.* Today, Renault is one of the largest manufacturers of front wheel drive vehicles in the world, with more than seventeen million

of them on the road.

Le Car also features rack-and-pinion steering — so precise and responsive that it's used in virtually every car built for competitive racing. Its double-triangle independent front suspension is unique in the industry, and its rear suspension is, according to *Car and Driver* magazine, "The single best rear suspension layout for front wheel drive cars...".

For 1980, Le Car has a new fuel-efficient 1.4 Liter engine coupled with a fully synchronized 4-speed manual transmission to

provide positive driving control and spontaneous pick-up power when you need it. Standard Michelin steel belted radials provide long tire life and offer exceptional tracking stability and skid resistance.

Powerful, self-adjusting disc brakes up front (power assisted on Le Car Deluxe) and double-leading shoe rear drum brakes contribute towards reliable, straight-line stops.

Exhilarating performance, decisive handling and remarkable comfort are only part of the Renault Le Car story for 1980.

H. *New, biomechanically engineered bucket seats in leatherette are standard on Le Car. The low-back front and rear seats were engineered to decrease driving fatigue and maximize driver and passenger comfort. The front seats lift and tilt forward in one easy motion*

for convenient rear seat access. Fully reclining bucket seats are standard on Le Car Deluxe. I. *Standard Michelin XZX steel belted radial tires mounted on styled wheels provide maximum wear, good handling and excellent traction and stability.* J. *Le Car's smart*

new instrument panel conveniently positions all switches and controls within easy access and visibility of the driver. Column mounted controls include windshield washers and wipers, headlights, "silent horn" headlight flasher, turn indicators and horn.

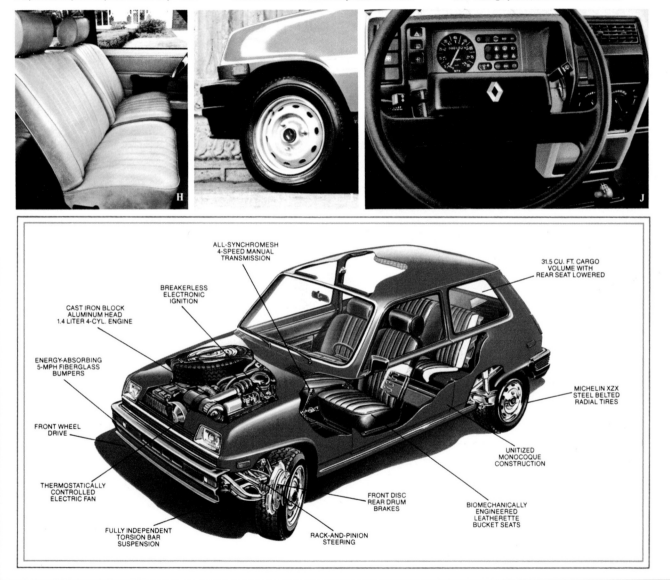

INTRODUCTION / HISTORY SPREAD, AMC / RENAULT
LeCAR CATALOG

This is another complex page spread from an automotive catalog. I was to depict some of the highlights in the history of Renault, and a good deal of research was required before I could even begin my layout. The client wanted the spread to illustrate the company's innovative ideas and show their extensive involvement in the automotive industry. After gathering enough reference material from various books and magazines, I was able to determine which items could be included. It was important to include a picture of Louis Renault, as well as pictures of some of the early competitive racing cars. I had pictures of some early Renault posters which would also add interest to the pages. An engineering drawing of an early transmission design and pictures of several important car models would complete the story.

IDEA-ROUGH SKETCH. This is my first idea rough, which I did in color, in an attempt to organize all of the material on the spread. It was imperative to get something in this form down on paper so the problem could be evaluated properly. I felt that the old poster was shown too large here and that some of the other items could have been rearranged into a more pleasing composition. It just didn't work as well as I had envisioned it. This is the real value of doing rough sketches for evaluation.

PRELIMINARY ROUGH SKETCH. I did another rough, this time a little more carefully, so that I could present it for discussion with my client before going any farther. The rough was done with a fine-line marker and colored Magic Markers on layout paper. I added two old posters and changed the size relationships of some of the elements, making the composition more pleasing. The client was quite satisfied with the way the spread was developing, and I proceeded with the comprehensive layout.

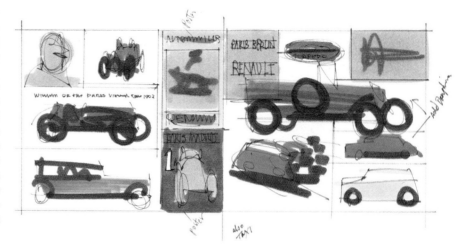

UNDERLAY DRAWING (left). My client called to tell me to add a Renault Dauphine as well as an old taxicab. After locating reference material for these cars, I made an underlay drawing with a fine-line marker pen on tracing paper. I drew some of the items by projecting the reference photos directly onto the paper and tracing the images. This drawing finalized the relative sizes of all of the elements and the general composition of the spread.

PRELIMINARY COLOR ROUGH (below). Because of the many items shown on this spread, I felt that it would simplify matters a great deal if I did a rough sketch to determine which colors would be used on the finished layout. As you can see, in spite of the fact that this sketch lacks detail, it still works well as a color guide. This sketch also was shown to the client, and a couple of small revisions were suggested—dropping the Dauphine model, adding a front-wheel-drive car, and the front view of a 1935 Primaquatre.

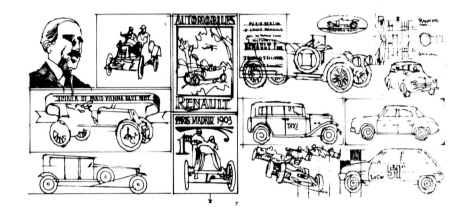

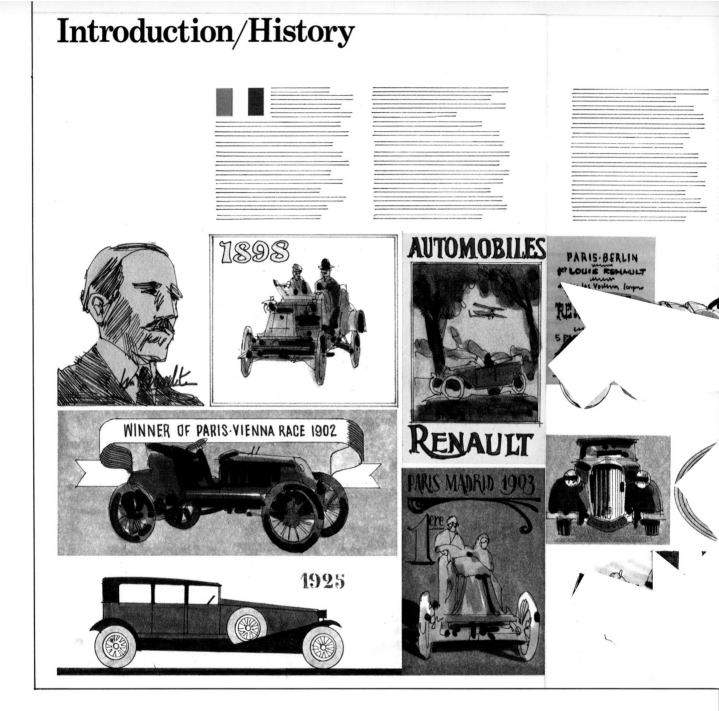

COMPREHENSIVE LAYOUT. After doing the underlay drawings for the new additions I proceeded to do the comprehensive layout in my usual manner. I traced the underlay drawing onto a sheet of layout paper with a technical pen. I drew the portrait of Renault with a slightly heavier line for the accents, using a Pentel pen. Then I rendered the drawings, using my previous color sketch as a guide. I put in the background colors for the Paris-Berlin poster and the transmission drawing by using a sheet of Letratone color tint overlay. Some of the fine lettering was done with a fine-line marker pen, and the colored letters were drawn with Prismacolor pencils. I put in the headline with Letraset transfer letters and ruled in the body copy with a technical pen.

PRINTED CATALOG HISTORY SPREAD. This is the history spread as it appeared in the printed catalog. It is very close to my comprehensive layout, and only a few minor changes are evident. Some of the colors have been changed, a different poster has been used, and a photograph has been substituted for the line drawing of Louis Renault. The finished art consists of the combined efforts of Mary Rupp, Ron Barry, and Craig Wilson, all illustrators working in the Detroit area. These catalogs were all produced for Wayne Alexander and Company of Bloomfield Hills, Michigan.

Renault: A Tradition of Outstanding Performance

EIGHT-PAGE BOOKLET FOR TENNA-TECH

This assignment was complex, as it involved the design of a booklet, a company logo, and artwork, as well as the necessary photography. The logo design was also to be incorporated into the cover design in some way. Tenna-Tech is a company involved in coal mining; it specializes in strip mining and land reclamation. This was a particularly interesting project for me, as I knew nothing about coal or about strip mining. Before I even began to think about the layout of the booklet or the logo design, I was asked to fly down to Tennessee to observe and photograph the company's operations. Eventually some of these photographs would be used in the proposed booklet, and they also would serve as visual references for the necessary artwork. This is contrary to the way assignments ordinarily are done. Usually the layout is produced first, and then the photographs are taken. After spending two hectic days photographing the company's operations, I came back to my studio and began designing the booklet.

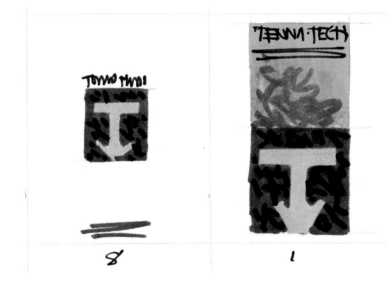

PRELIMINARY ROUGH SKETCHES. These roughs are of the front and rear covers of the booklet. On the rear cover I used a rough rendition of the proposed company logo, a stylized *T* with an arrow on the end, superimposed on a background photograph of coal. On the front cover I also showed the logo design, but directly above it I indicated a photograph of very young trees, symbolizing the land which the company reclaims after its strip-mining operations are finished.

PRELIMINARY ROUGH SKETCHES. On pages 2 and 3 of the booklet, I was to show just how the strip-mining operation is performed and how the land is reclaimed. I felt that the best way to show this would be through the use of a painted diagrammatic illustration, as it would be too difficult to show through photography. The strip-mining diagram would be in three sections: the first would show the coal being exposed, the next section would depict the working of the exposed coal seams, and the third section would demonstrate the reclamation process. The other page on this spread would be composed of photographs of the bulldozers at work removing the soil from the coal seams.

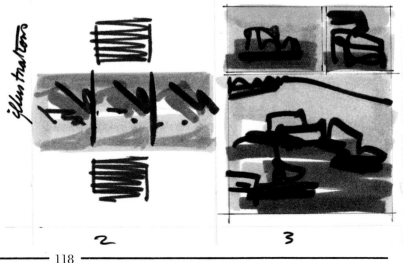

4

5

6

7 WHITE BORDER

PRELIMINARY ROUGH SKETCHES. These are the preliminary rough sketches for the other pages in the booklet. After deciding which photographs best told the story, I was able to complete this rough. On page 7 is a map that shows how the coal barges reach the Gulf of Mexico for overseas shipment. You can see how simply this story is told, with only artwork, photographs, and a few simple captions. I was not required to produce another layout for this piece; instead, I prepared the artwork for the printer from the preliminary rough layouts.

Rotary drill installs shot holes in the shale deposit. After blasting, front-end loaders work the exposed coal seam.

Coal is crushed, processed, and sized for various industrial uses.

After processing, coal is loaded on trucks for transportation to river barges where it is moved by closed conveyor into the barges.

Barges waiting for tugs to transport them down river for ocean ship transfer.

FINISHED BOOKLET. Here is the completed piece, which shows how the Tenna-Tech logo was incorporated into the front cover design. The logo works very well and combines nicely with all of the other photographs, something which had to be considered when I was designing this piece. The photographs were all taken with a Nikon Ftn reflex camera using 50mm, 24mm, and 135mm telephoto lenses.

BROCHURE COVER FOR PREMIER CORPORATION

I was asked by James Donahue, Advertising Manager of Premier Corporation, to design a brochure cover symbolizing the company's operations, which include ranches, farming, cattle ranges, meat packing, and cattle breeding. He wanted a distinctive, colorful, contemporary design with illustrations of the various company functions. In my file I had many photographs that I had taken while on a visit to Premier, and I was able to refer to these when doing the layout.

IDEA-ROUGH SKETCHES. When I first thought about this problem and did the idea rough on the left, I felt that perhaps the best solution would be to show each company operation in a separate color panel. This did not seem to hold together well, however, and so I tried another concept, using the pictures of the company operations over a series of color stripes. This arrangement worked very well, and I decided to try a larger, more detailed rough of this version.

PRELIMINARY ROUGH SKETCHES. This is the new rough I made, using the stripe motif. At the top I indicated a bull; next, a ranch scene with a cowboy; a scene of cattle on the range; a farm scene; and farm equipment. My indications of these scenes appear as scribbles, but they are still based on specific photographic reference material. This rough worked quite well, but I felt it needed a little more white space on the page, and so I decided to revise it. In the new version (right), I kept the colored section of the design on the lower half of the page, leaving the upper section blank except for the headline.

SEMI-COMPREHENSIVE LAYOUT. I did this full-size semi-comp for presentation to the client. I did the illustrations by working up the underlay drawing first and then tracing it onto a sheet of layout paper with a Pilot Fineliner pen. Then I added the colors with Magic Markers and rendered the lettering with black and gray Prismacolor pencils.

PRINTED BROCHURE COVER. Here is the finished, printed brochure cover. The artwork was drawn on illustration board with India ink and a technical pen. The grays were washes of water-soluble ink. The color was added by the printer, who used my layout and a keyline which I prepared as a guide. A keyline is an exact-size mechanical drawing which the printer uses to make the printing plates. This drawing or guide usually has type mounted in place and shows the correct sizes and placement of artwork or photographs.

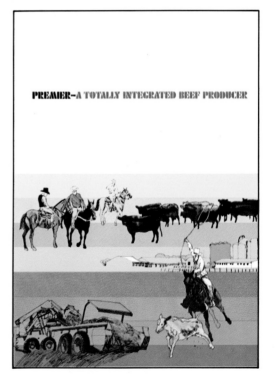

TV STORYBOARDS

These two storyboard assignments were from Lintas/Paris. One was for Karting, a clothing manufacturer, and the other for Kit Kat candy. For each commercial, I was given rough idea sketches which clearly depicted the sequence of the film's action. TV storyboards are presented to the clients for approval, after which live-action films, based on these visuals, are produced.

IDEA-ROUGH SKETCHES. This assignment sheet from Lintas was for a Kit Kat candy commercial. This was one of a series of three storyboards I produced for them. These diagrams helped me a great deal when I was working up the TV frames.

TV STORYBOARD COMPREHENSIVE LAYOUT. The finished storyboard frames were done in a fast, simple technique that is suited for producing a great number of frames.

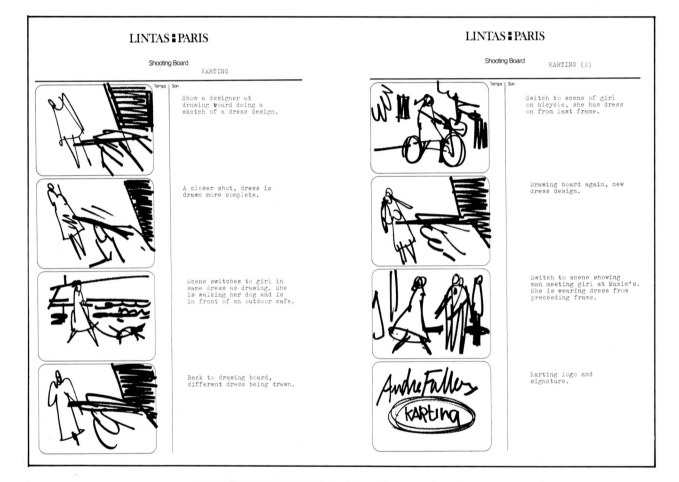

IDEA-ROUGH SKETCHES. In this assignment sheet for Karting, Pierre Rosenthal, Creative Director of Lintas/ Paris, wanted to convey the idea of a dress designer at work sketching his creations and then the scene shifting to a photograph of a woman wearing the same dress. I was to do eight full-color renderings depicting this action. The simple rough sketches on the assignment sheet were a great help, as the visual idea that the art director had in his mind was quite clear.

TV STORYBOARD COMPREHENSIVE LAYOUT (opposite page). These are the finished TV storyboard frames. I did them simply, using a fine-line pen and colored Magic Markers.

TYPICAL ASSIGNMENTS

ADVERTISING LAYOUT

COMPANY LOGO DESIGN AND MAGAZINE AD SERIES FOR
LAFAYETTE RE

When I originally accepted this assignment, I was asked to design just a company logo for Lafayette Re, a Paris-based insurance company. They accepted one of my proposals for the logo and then asked me to design a series of magazine ads as well. They were interested in developing a very strong image through these ads, something readers would remember easily.

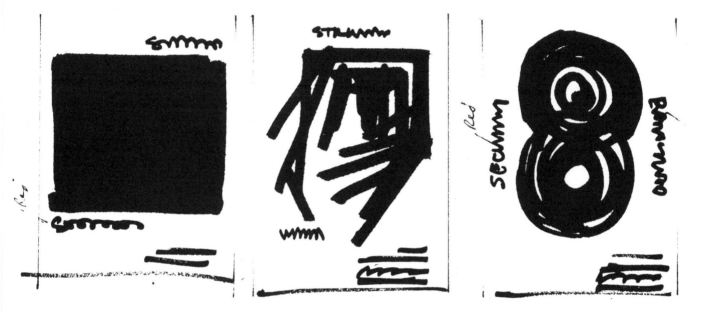

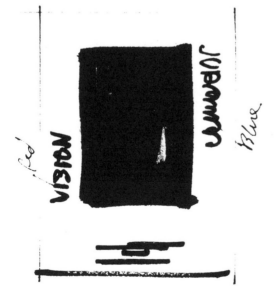

IDEA-ROUGH SKETCHES. When I began thinking about this series of ads, I felt the solution might come from my new painting direction, which was very strong visually. I worked up these roughs and decided this was the way to proceed with the campaign. These idea roughs are very small, 2⅜″ x 3⅛″ (6 x 8 cm), but they still convey the design feeling I was after. For the headlines, I decided on a few key words which describe the company, and I worked up the comprehensive layouts with photocopies of the paintings mounted in position.

VISION

Mead Reassurances S.A.

Lafayette Re

16 AVENUE DE MESSINE 75008 PARIS FRANCE TEL 256 20 80 TELEX 642297 F

FINISHED ADS. The layouts were presented to the company president, Robert W. Virtue, and he liked the campaign very much. Shown here and on page 132 are four of the ads in the series, some of which may be reproduced as posters in the future. Incidentally, the company liked the paintings enough to purchase the ones used, and they are now hanging in the company offices.

EXPERIENCE

Mead Reassurances S.A.

Lafayette Re

16 AVENUE DE MESSINE 75008 PARIS FRANCE TEL 256 20 80 TELEX 642297 F

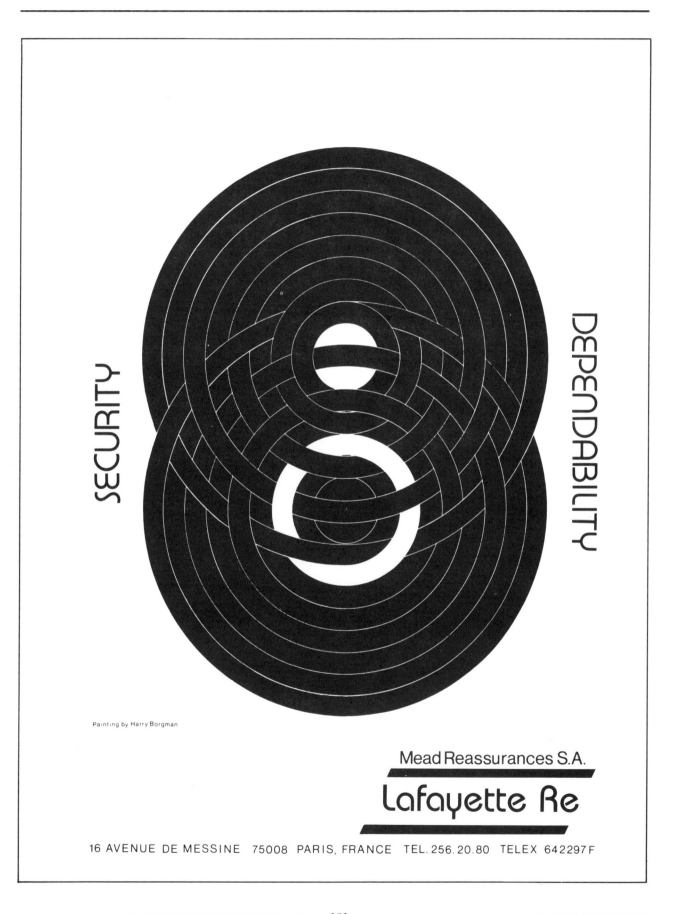

SECURITY

DEPENDABILITY

Painting by Harry Borgman

Mead Reassurances S.A.

Lafayette Re

16 AVENUE DE MESSINE 75008 PARIS, FRANCE TEL. 256.20.80 TELEX 642297 F

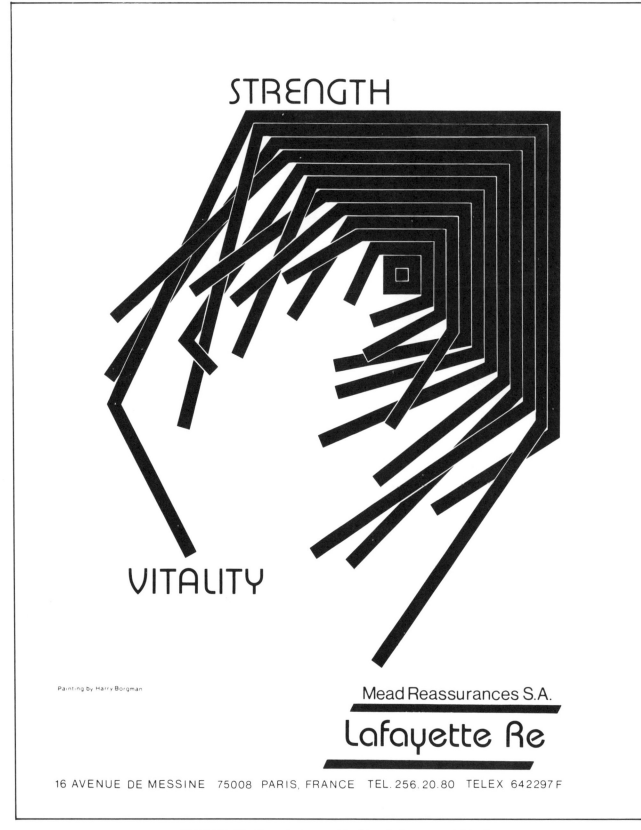

STRENGTH

VITALITY

Painting by Harry Borgman

Mead Reassurances S.A.

Lafayette Re

16 AVENUE DE MESSINE   75008 PARIS, FRANCE   TEL. 256.20.80   TELEX 642297 F

FINISHED AD. The painting used in this ad also was exhibited in the Salon de Mai in Paris. It is entitled *A Square, Self-Destructing,* is painted on canvas with acrylic paint, and measures 44⅞'' x 63¾'' (114 x 162 cm).

MAGAZINE AD FOR ROCHAS MACASSAR

In this assignment I was to develop only the picture composition and content, not the actual design of the ad. Art Director Jean-Michel Gasquét, of Impact/FCB in Paris, wanted an Indonesian setting for the background scene. The picture was to show a couple meeting on the stairs in the background, and a large statue or carving in the foreground area. It was also suggested that I put a servant in the scene.

IDEA-ROUGH SKETCHES. These idea roughs helped me to establish the picture composition. Simple sketches like these help to establish one's thinking on how to organize the picture space, what emphasis should be put on which objects in the scene, and even the lighting in the proposed situation. I felt that a foreground object would help the composition in the first sketch. The art director had suggested a carving, and so I tried another rough using a large statue, which worked quite well. I developed this idea a little further with another sketch, using a few gray marker tones. This seemed to work very well as a solution to the composition of the scene.

PENCIL DRAWING FOR APPROVAL. The art director asked me to submit a pencil sketch of my composition before going ahead with the finished comprehensive layout. Using the final idea-rough sketch as a basis, I did a tight pencil drawing of the scene on tracing paper. This pencil sketch was detailed enough so that everyone concerned could see how the illustration was developing. It was decided that the statue in the foreground should be emphasized, the man should be taller, and both figures should appear in white clothing. The figure of the servant was thought to be too distracting and was to be eliminated.

COMPREHENSIVE LAYOUT RENDERING. Here is the finished layout rendering, which incorporates all of the suggestions and changes. This rendering was done primarily with gray Magic Marker tones and gray, white, and black Prismacolor pencils on layout paper. This rendering was mounted into a layout with the headlines and type and presented to the client along with several other ad proposals. The ad was accepted, and a photographer was hired to take the photograph, basing the scene on this sketch.

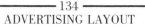

TYPICAL ASSIGNMENTS

MACASSAR

LE NOUVEAU ROCHAS POUR HOMME

ROCHAS
PARIS

FINISHED AD. Here is the ad as it appeared in the publications. It is quite different from the sketch that was approved. You can see that it was decided to eliminate the Indonesian statue, perhaps because of the difficulty of locating such an object. In addition, the figures were placed much closer to the foreground and the table was pushed to the background. Often an ad undergoes changes like this in the final photographic session. The art director or photographer might think of last-minute alterations, as happened in this case. Occasionally several versions of the same scene are shot and the client chooses the photograph that best suits the ad. This photograph was taken by Francis Giacobetti of Paris.

MAGAZINE AD FOR CANON

My role in this assignment was to render the illustration and not be concerned with the design of the ad, which was done by the art director. This black-and-white double spread was part of a series of ads produced at the same time. Most advertisements are produced as part of a series or campaign and are presented to the client in this manner. The advertising agency art directors generally design these ads but rely on outside services for making the finished renderings and assembling the ads for presentation.

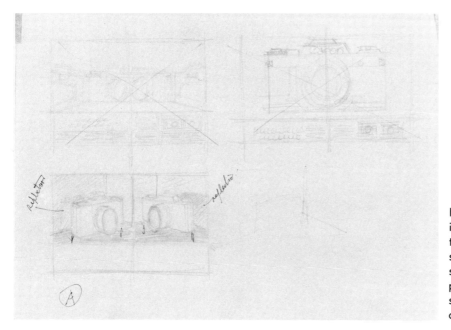

IDEA-ROUGH SKETCHES. These small idea roughs were done by the art director to show me exactly how he envisioned the ads. These sketches may seem quite crude, but with a verbal explanation, they were sufficient as a starting point for developing the ad campaign.

UNDERLAY DRAWING. I was given the product by the art director, and this enabled me to take Polaroid photographs, which I could then project to the correct size for doing my underlay drawing on tracing paper. You can see that this drawing is quite rough, but the proportions are accurate enough to enable me to produce a precise drawing of the camera.

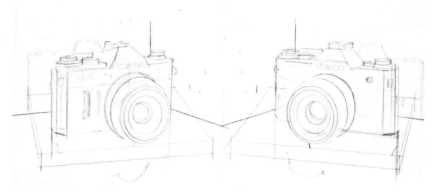

COMPREHENSIVE LAYOUT RENDER-ING (above). Next I traced the underlay drawing onto a sheet of layout paper with a fine-line marker. As I drew, I re-ferred to my Polaroid photograph so that the various details on the camera would be accurate. When the basic out-line drawing had been completed, I be-gan to add the marker tones, starting out with the background and the lighter values on the product. I gradually built up the darker tones and finally added the deep black accents. The bright high-lights were painted in with a brush and permanent white designers' gouache. This finished rendering was mounted into the layout, complete with type and headline, and was presented to the client with the rest of the series.

FINISHED AD (left). After the layout was approved by the client, the advertising agency hired a photographer to photo-graph the products, using my layout ren-derings as a basis for the composition and feeling.

Le Canon AE 1... L'appareil reflex le plus vendu dans le monde, déjà 4 millions d'exemplaires.   *Le Canon AE 1 Program... Comme une voiture à option, il propose, pour un jeu plus cher, quelques services en plus.*

Canon AE 1... ou Canon AE 1?..

NEWSPAPER AD SERIES FOR TRANSCONTINENTAL TRAVEL BUREAU

Small newspaper ads can be quite a challenge to a designer, especially when the ads appear on newspaper pages crowded with other ads, such as you see in the Sunday travel section. My objective in doing these particular ads was to make them stand out strongly among the competition.

PRELIMINARY ROUGH LAYOUT. This preliminary rough layout was presented to my client for approval. It was easy for me to convey exactly what I had in mind for this ad campaign because I had drawn one of the hotels that would appear in the ads, enabling the client to see the exact style I proposed for the artwork. The drawing was done on the special-surfaced illustration board called scratchboard. Ink drawings can be done on this surface and a special tool used to scratch out white lines and clean up the edges.

FINISHED AD. This is the finished ad as it appeared in the newspapers. Note how little it has changed from the original rough layout; the basic feeling is exactly the same. It was not necessary for me to develop the layouts for these ads to the comprehensive stage, as the client was able to visualize clearly what I had in mind from the preliminary roughs.

FINISHED AD. You can see just how closely the finished ad corresponds to the preliminary rough layout. This is because I was given the exact information on the number of elements to appear in the ads. The short copy blocks were written to fit the spaces allowed for them on the layout.

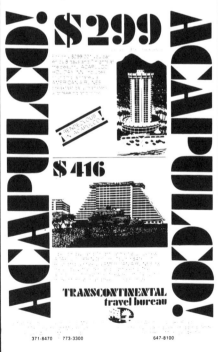

GETTING STARTED IN THIS FIELD

After reading this book, you should be more aware of what is involved in working as a layout-rendering artist. It should be clear that to be successful in this field, you must develop a clean, fresh rendering style as well as a faculty for working quickly under pressure. These are capabilities which can be acquired through practice and experience.

You can practice on your own, of course, but how do you get the experience? A person interested in a career in layout rendering can begin by applying for a job as an apprentice in a commercial art studio or advertising agency. Among other duties, a basic requirement is that the apprentice cut mats, mount layouts, and prepare other artwork for presentation. This position enables the beginner to work directly with professional illustrators and renderers, observing firsthand just how different assignments are produced. An apprentice can move up from the mat room by developing rendering skills and becoming an apprentice artist.

Jobs for apprentices are available, but there is a great deal of competition for them. When applying for an apprentice position, you must do everything you can to prove to the employer that you have potential as an artist. Ad agencies and art studios are interested in hiring personnel they feel have the ambition and ability to move up into higher positions as layout renderers or illustrators. Since many young artists are after these jobs, you must put together a well-rounded portfolio of your work to present when you apply.

Also try to get into contact with other beginners, particularly anyone who is already working as an apprentice. This kind of contact will benefit you a great deal, as you will be able to learn about the business and perhaps be able to examine professional work firsthand. Read as much as you can about the business; there are trade publications, books, and business-related magazines available at your local art supply store and in the public library. It is good to remember that most of your competition are other artists who take more than a casual interest in all areas of art. You should be interested in and informed about fine art as well as commercial art. Make regular visits to galleries, local museums, and advertising and fine art exhibitions so you will be aware of what is going on.

You can develop yourself in other areas of art, perhaps by enrolling in a life-drawing class in the evenings or on Saturdays. Practice doing small drawings or paintings while vacationing or traveling, as this will contribute greatly to your development as an artist.

I have especially enjoyed the personal freedom and independence this field of work has afforded me. I have worked on my own as a freelance artist for many years, working for clients in the United States, Europe, and the Far East. There is no doubt that advertising layout is a very special business with unusual opportunities. If this kind of a career appeals to you and suits your personality, you should consider it seriously. Along with many interesting challenges, this very stimulating business also offers the opportunity for personal growth.

INDEX